IMAGES
of America

HARLEM TOWNSHIP IN WINNEBAGO COUNTY

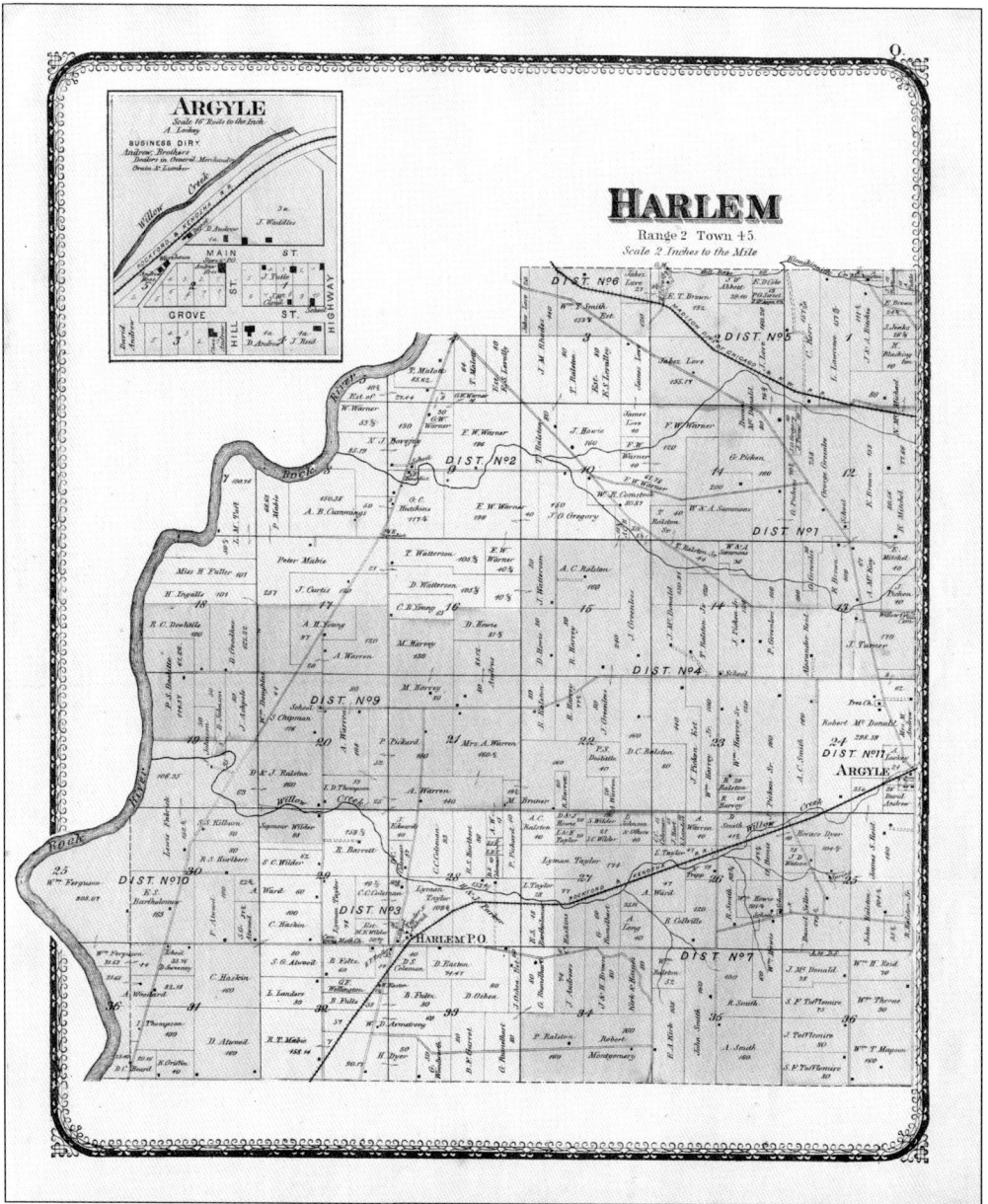

Harlem Township was established on November 6, 1849. This map of the township is from 1871. Today, Harlem Township has approximately 40,000 inhabitants and is the second most populated township in Winnebago County after Rockford Township. The total area is 33.38 square miles. (Courtesy of Brian Landis.)

ON THE COVER: Almost all rural communities had creameries, and Harlem was no exception. The creamery at Harlem was built in 1882 by F. Stevenson on the south side of Harlem Road between Harlem Hills Road (Forest Hills Road) and Middle Road (Alpine Road). It supplied Harlem with milk products such as cheese and butter, and was destroyed by fire in 1913. This photograph is from around 1900. (Courtesy of Brian Landis)

IMAGES
of America

HARLEM TOWNSHIP IN WINNEBAGO COUNTY

Tim McGrew with Brian Landis

ARCADIA
PUBLISHING

Copyright © 2020 by Tim McGrew and Brian Landis
ISBN 978-1-4671-0443-2

Published by Arcadia Publishing
Charleston, South Carolina

Printed in the United States of America

Library of Congress Control Number: 2019944902

For all general information, please contact Arcadia Publishing:
Telephone 843-853-2070
Fax 843-853-0044
E-mail sales@arcadiapublishing.com
For customer service and orders:
Toll-Free 1-888-313-2665

Visit us on the Internet at www.arcadiapublishing.com

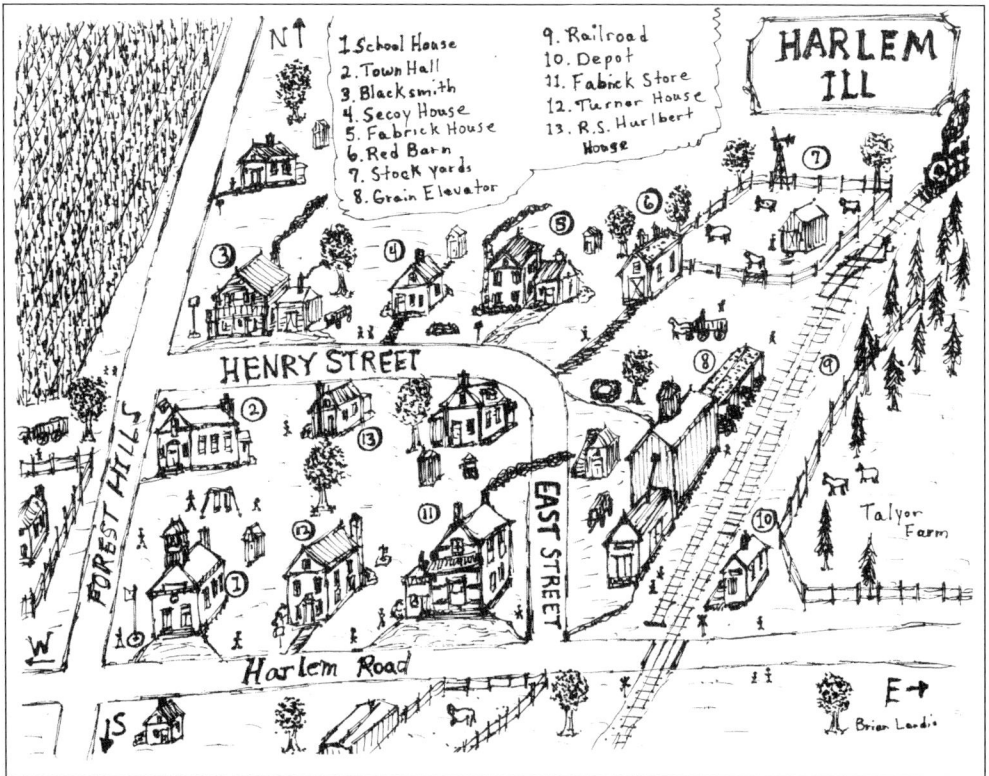

This hand-drawn map depicts Harlem village around the 1890s. The village of Harlem was typical of many small communities of the day—it provided the basic needs of a rural community. Very little remains of the village today. (Map drawn by Brian Landis.)

CONTENTS

ACKNOWLEDGMENTS

It has been a unique opportunity to assemble an extensive record of information, photographs, and memorabilia for this publication about Harlem Township in Winnebago County. But what is truly remarkable is that one man, Brian Landis, has been tirelessly compiling such a record for decades. His dedication and resourcefulness in the study of local history cannot be overstated. Much of this publication's content is comprised of his collection of historical photographs. With that being said, it is even more remarkable that so many others have given freely of their time, resources, and knowledge to make this publication possible. We are extremely grateful and honored to have the following organizations and individuals contribute to this endeavor. The order of contributors is by no means reflective of the quantity or importance of their contribution, for every single photograph preserved is a testament to our ancestors and our heritage.

I would graciously like to thank the following organizations: Vintage Aerial, Midway Village Museum, Rockford Public Library Local History Room and Jean Lythgoe, North Suburban District Library, Harlem School District, Harlem Township, North Park Fire Department, North Park Evangelical Covenant Church, North Park University, Rockford Speedway, First Baptist Church of Machesney Park, and the Kewanee Historical Society. In addition, I would like to thank the following individuals: Gene Anderson, Rose Bennett, Jackie Chamberlain, Howard Easton, Iva Hansen, Kevin Jacobson, William L. Johnson, Scott Landis, Jennifer Paulson, Rory and Cedric Peterson, Jeanine Pumilia, JoAnn Reid, Jim Rezich, and Barb Speiser. We would also like to thank Arcadia Publishing, our editor Angel Hisnanick, and Jeff Ruetsche for the opportunity to present this publication to the citizens of Harlem Township.

In addition to photographs, the following people have contributed a lifetime's worth of research and historical knowledge: Ed Carlson, Terry Johnson, Robert Ralston, and Don Sonneson.

Please note that every effort was made to attribute the photographs in this publication to their original sources. However, it is sometimes difficult, if not impossible, to obtain the original sources of photographs taken decades ago. If you find material in here that can be attributed to the original source or you are the original source, please contact the writer and/or publisher, and every effort will be made to include corrections in subsequent printings.

INTRODUCTION

The story of this region really starts with the Native American Indians and the French, because when the early settlers came into this region, there was still ample evidence of their habitation in the area. The last Native Americans to call the area of Harlem Township home were the Winnebago Indians. In a 1914 newspaper article, Anna Parker was still able to point out the Indian trails that went from her farm (Section 28 of Harlem Township) off into Rock Cut. The rock formation in Rock Cut State Park known as "Lone Rock" was said to be a ceremonial location for the Winnebago who camped there. There were French traders in the region long before the area was officially settled. They conducted trade with Native Americans in the area until after the conclusion of the Revolutionary War in 1783. There was a French-Indian settlement in the area just outside of Ledges Golf Course on the Kinnikinnick Creek, just a few miles north of Harlem Township. French traders often bored holes in trees to tap them for sap. As late as the early 20th century, trees have been found in the region with boreholes made by the French—some of these are in the area of present-day Rock Cut State Park.

Illinois officially became a state in 1818. It was populated from south to north, with the formation of counties extending northward. The last Indian war fought east of the Mississippi was in this region in 1832. Though it only lasted months, it came to be known as the Black Hawk War. After it ended in 1832, settlers started to trickle into the area of Winnebago County and what would later become Harlem Township. In 1836, Winnebago County was officially organized, and settlers started arriving from the East in great numbers. Most of the early settlers of Harlem Township came from New York and Scotland, making this area a cultural extension of the communities they left. Harlem is named for Harlem, New York, and Argyle after Argyllshire, Scotland. As for the Indians, most of them had been driven west into Iowa. But some bands of Winnebago used this area as their wintering and ceremonial grounds. There are accounts of early settlers in the area who saw some Winnebago here into the late 1840s.

Hiram Wattles made a failed attempt at starting a settlement on the east banks of the Rock River. He staked out lots and streets on a chunk of land in an area known as "Big Bottom." Wattles chose to call his town Scipio. His house was the only one ever built, and the town never materialized for reasons that can only be speculated upon, but the name Big Bottom may offer a clue. This was the name used by the Native Americans to describe the low-lying area along the east bank of the Rock River. Much of this area eventually became Harlem Township. The Big Bottom area extends from just south of Loves Park to just north of Roscoe. The area around Martin Park in Loves Park, Shore Drive in Machesney Park, and Roscoe in Atwood Park has seen extensive flooding for as long as it has been settled.

Hiram Wattles was not the only one to pin hopes on building a town in Harlem Township. There is a little-known but fascinating story among local historians. Buried deep in the woods of Rock Cut State Park on what was once the Charles Parker residence, there was a building called the Buckhorn Tavern. If local newspaper accounts and Charles A. Church's *History of*

Rockford and Winnebago County are correct, this would have been the oldest tavern in Winnebago County. Some even claim that this was the oldest building in the county. Taverns of that era varied in the amount of services they offered. These were inns where a traveler could spend the night and put up their horses. They often provided a meal, traveling provisions, and a place to rest and socialize. The Buckhorn was so popular that the stagecoach made a special trip off the main road (Belvidere to Beloit) and traveled through the woods to get there. It was said to have had two additions. A Mr. Sammons was the first owner and hoped that a town would spring up there. A 1914 newspaper account said that this building was 100 years old at that time. That early date has never been validated and seems rather unlikely. There were, however, tavern licenses granted in the area at least as early as 1838—two years after the first roads were surveyed in Winnebago County.

Settlers coming into Harlem Township faced many challenges in getting here. Prairie grass was several feet tall. Grass reeds were wound around wagon wheels to help ford the creeks in the area. Roads were very primitive and difficult to navigate. They went point-to-point between destinations—often diagonally. When the township form of government was adopted (1849–1850), most of the early roads were rerouted to township section lines. By the 1830s, Buffalo were a rare sight in the region. According to accounts by early settlers, one of the last remaining herds grazed in the region of Argyle along the Winnebago and Boone County line. There were still black bear, mountain lions, wolves, and rattlesnakes to contend with, along with a plethora of other wildlife.

Anyone exploring the early history of Harlem Township continues to run across the same family names over and over again. Many of these families intermarried with other settler families, creating and preserving a lasting pioneer heritage. Some of these names include Andrus, Armour, Atwood, Bartholomew, Dyer, Doolittle, Easton, Evans, Fabrick, Ferguson, Greenlee, Hall, Haskin, Hurlbert, Parker, Paulson, Picken, Ralston, Reid, Rogers, Rumelhart, Swarthout, Taylor, and others. This list is by no means inclusive of all the early settlers of Harlem Township—there are many others.

Harlem Village, like so many other early villages, was somewhat transitory. Some historians believe that Harlem may have had three different locations, while others claim two different locations. The first location for Harlem Village is thought to have been on North Alpine Road (then called Middle Road), where Willow Creek runs. This is approximately in the area of Harlem High School. There was a post office, tavern (stagecoach stop), school, and horse stables just to the north. A post office gave merit to it being an established community. The only building that survives from this first location is a restored home at 9124 North Alpine Road. It dates to 1838 and may have been a stagecoach stop. Anything else that remained of this first townsite was torn down in the 1950s. There are some who claim that the second site of Harlem was at Harlem and Alpine Roads. This is where Asa Taylor donated land for a school, church, and cemetery. While this was certainly a hub of activity and a key location in the history of Harlem, it by no means indicates that the town of Harlem was ever officially located here. There is nothing official (such as a post office) that points to this being the second location of Harlem. The next location, however, is well documented. In 1859, the Kenosha & Rockford Railroad was formed. It became apparent that the railroad would run diagonally across the southern and middle portion of Harlem Township and turn east. For this reason, the town of Harlem was moved to Harlem Road and Forest Hills. At this location, there would be a school, town hall, grain elevator, general store, the Harlem train depot, stockyards, a blacksmith shop, a creamery, and several homes.

Argyle was settled by the Armour brothers first in 1834, then the Greenlee family (1836), the Reid family (1837), the Picken family (1839), and the Ralston family (1841), as well as others. When the railroad went through in 1859, it was built by Irishmen from Wisconsin.

Argyle, like Harlem, had a depot on the Kenosha & Rockford Railroad (KD). The railroad was bought by the Chicago & North Western (CNW) in 1861 and became the Kenosha Division of the CNW (KD line). There were initially 10–12 trains a day between Rockford and Harvard, although that number varied over the years. Although the railroad was a core component of Harlem Township, neither the village of Harlem nor the village of Argyle became a successful business center on par with some other communities. In 1902, the Rockford, Beloit, & Janesville electric interurban railroad was built parallel to North Second Street. The site of the new Harlem Consolidated School was chosen at Harlem Road and North Second Street for this reason. It afforded students in outlying areas the ability to get to school on public transportation. The line was discontinued this far north in 1930, and by 1936, it was entirely gone in Rockford.

Harlem Township, despite the fact that it never developed large towns or cities, was nevertheless very successful. It has become a powerhouse in terms of attractions. What was once a Winnebago Indian campground became Rock Cut Forest Preserve when the Winnebago County Forest Preserve District was organized in 1922 and began adding parks in 1924. It then became an Illinois state park beginning in 1956. Today, Rock Cut State Park draws thousands of visitors from all around, including Chicago and its suburbs.

Just down the street from Rock Cut State Park is the Rockford Speedway, which has been thrilling race fans since 1948. It is one of only two NASCAR sanctioned tracks in Illinois, with the other being in Joliet.

Harlem Township became the second most-populated township in Winnebago County, next to Rockford. The name Harlem lives on in so many ways that it is almost impossible to draw up a complete list of all the place names utilizing it. There is the Harlem School District, Harlem High School, Harlem Road, Harlem Community Center, Harlem Township, and others. With that being said, it is important to note that much of the area that is within Harlem Township was once an unincorporated area called North Park. It had this name for decades until North Park became incorporated and the name was officially changed to Machesney Park in 1981. There are still public entities that use the North Park name, such as the North Park Fire Department and the North Park Public Water District. There are also a few private enterprises that still use the North Park name.

But North Park is not the only name that has been used to describe businesses or business locations in Harlem Township. The first Rockford airport was, in fact, in Harlem Township. Fred Machesney's airport was referred to as Rockford Airport until the Greater Rockford Airport Board was formed in 1947 and Rockford Airport was opened south of the city of Rockford. Rockford Speedway is in Harlem Township. Over the years, there have been many things in Harlem Township that were referred to as being in Rockford. The reasons for this are because the area was unincorporated for so long, and it has a close proximity to Rockford. Similarly, today, the current Rockford Airport is referred to as Chicago-Rockford Airport because of its proximity to Chicago.

It is quite a challenge to encapsulate the history of schools in Harlem School District 122. The reason for this is that the Harlem School District actually lies in two different townships: Harlem and Rockford (formerly Guilford). This publication is only focused on the schools that are physically within Harlem Township. For that reason, there are no photographs of Harlem High School on Windsor Road, Loves Park Grade School, and Marshal Middle School. This is not meant to overlook their historical importance but rather to limit the scope of this book to Harlem Township. It is also important to note that the boundaries of Loves Park and Machesney Park, Harlem Township, and Rockford Township have fluctuated over time due to annexations and boundary disputes. There are some streets in the area that have blocks that lie within both townships. What was once in Harlem Township and North Park might currently be in Rockford Township and Loves Park, or vice versa.

The center of Harlem Township's business district is still transitory to this day. The focal point of the township was once on North Alpine Road, in the 9100 block. Then it moved to the area of Forest Hills and Harlem Roads. Then it moved to West Harlem, which was the intersection of Harlem Road and North Second Street. When the Machesney Park Mall opened in 1978, that became the focal point of Harlem. Now, we have a new focal point of Harlem Township, the Route 173 (West Lane) corridor.

As much as place names and addresses present a challenge, so do street names. For instance, Alpine Road was once called Middle Road because it lies between Forest Hills Road and Illinois 251. That highway has been called Beloit Road, Route 51, and North Second Street. Forest Hills Road was originally an ancient Indian trail. There is a historical marker in Antioch, Illinois, dedicated to the Native American ties to this route. Route 173 is also called West Lane, Ralston Road, and farther west, Latham Road. Forest Hills Road was also called Bluff Street in the village of Harlem, and going south from there, it was called Harlem Hills Road. Harlem Road was once called Church Street in and around the village of Harlem. In addition to these names, the early roads were also given rural route numbers, of which there are many. So, the next time you are walking or driving down one of these roads, think of the many people who have traversed these roads before you—some of them even before the historical era began.

The Huskies Drive-In Root Beer Barrel used to be located at the Machesney Airport and was a popular hangout spot (see page 71). After the airport closed in 1974, Huskies also closed, and the barrel was moved to its present location in the late 1970s. Once orange and black, it is now painted green.(Photograph by Brian Landis.)

One

HARLEM, ILLINOIS

This 1841 ad is for sections of land for sale by Eliakin Simons. Simons had purchased tracts of land in Sections 17, 28, 29, and 20, totaling some 200 acres in Harlem Township. Much of his land was along Willow Creek, where sections 20 and 29 meet. It is uncertain where Harlem Corners was located, but the area of present-day Harlem High School on Alpine Road seems plausible. At the time of first settlement, land sold for as little as $1 per acre and was usually purchased from the government. Once speculators came into the area, prices began to increase rapidly. Despite the increases, available land became scarce rather soon. The first land purchased was along the Rock River and Willow Creek. (Courtesy of Brian Landis.)

LAND O.

THE subscriber will sell all or any part of

1000 ACRES

Land lying on "BIG BOTTOM," and situated on WILLOW CREEK."

Said land has several improvements on it, amounting to about one hundred acres or more. One of about thirty acres; one of twenty-five, two of about twenty or more, all enclosed by good fence, and spring crops on all the ground. One of the improvements has on it a frame house and frame barn twenty-six by fifty-two, and a few fruit trees. "Willow Creek" runs through the whole length of the farm. One at "Harlem Corners" with a house part block and part frame with a small "NURSERY" of APPLE, PEACH, AND LOCUST. The other two improvements are immediately on the Section line, and so situated as to divide conveniently into two farms. All watered by the creek.

I will sell all or any part of the land with or without the crops at reasonable prices and give immediate possession.

There is a sufficient quantity of good timberland for the supply of the prairie.

☞ N. B. For further particulars enquire of the subscriber at Harlem Corners.

ELIAKIM SIMONS.

Harlem, May 29, 1841.

Built in 1838 at 9421 North Alpine Road, this property is thought to have been a stagecoach stop in the original Harlem Village. This has proven difficult to document, but one thing is for certain: this is the only building that still stands from the original Harlem Village. Across the street to the east stood the first Harlem Post Office. Nearby were government horse stables. (Courtesy of Vintage Aerial.)

This 1838 home is often referred to as "the Stage Coach Stop." The foundation consists of 18-inch-thick limestone. This property was saved from demolition and renovated by Donna Conley in 1965. Just to the south is Willow Creek. The proximity to the creek made this a prime location for early settlement. (Courtesy of Brian Landis.)

The Harlem grain elevator was built by F. Fabrick in 1888. In 1922, it was sold to J.H. Patterson Lumber Company. The CNW Kenosha Division line ran between the grain elevator and the Harlem Depot on the right. The Taylor Farm is in the background. This photograph was taken on December 18, 1917. (Courtesy of Midway Village Museum.)

The creamery at Harlem was built in 1882 by F. Stevenson and destroyed by fire in 1913. It was located on the south side of Harlem Road between Harlem Hills Road (Forest Hills Road) and Middle Road (Alpine Road). Today, this would be on the south side of Harlem Road approximately where Anna's Pizza is located. Local farmers brought their milk to creameries by wagon or train, where it was converted to cheese and other products. Less than a mile away, the KD line of the CNW Railroad served as a transportation route for local farmers. (Courtesy of Brian Landis.)

A necessity of any community in the 19th century was a blacksmith shop. This blacksmith shop was built in 1871 at the corner of Henry and Forest Hills Roads by Alfred Turner. (Courtesy of Midway Village Museum.)

The Harlem blacksmith shop was converted to an automobile repair garage in the 1920s, when the need for blacksmith shops was on the wane. This automobile repair shop was located where Sonneson Gas and Grocery was in the 1950s and where Subway was located until recently. (Courtesy of Midway Village Museum.)

This is the Harlem Store and post office. Isaac Swarthout (standing next to the carriage) was appointed postmaster on May 27, 1886. This store was built in 1871 by Thomas Fabrick. In 1928, it was destroyed by fire, and another store was erected in its place. Standing on the second-floor balcony is Louisa Swarthout and her daughter. In the buggy is Harriett (Swarthout) Hart and her baby Harold. (Courtesy of Midway Village Museum.)

The Easton family owned multiple tracts of land in Harlem Township. This farm on the south side of Harlem Road belonged to David Easton. Unfortunately, this beautiful farmhouse burned down. This 74-acre farm was midway between Forest Hills Road and present-day Perryville Road. (Courtesy of Midway Village Museum.)

There was more than one Easton family farm; one still stands today at Forest Hills and Windsor Roads. Easton family members in this 1918 photograph are, from left to right, unidentified grandparents, Glen (in goat cart), Roy, Lee, and Henry, who was the father of Howard Easton. (Courtesy of Brian Landis.)

This is the Easton farmhouse and barn (in back) on Forest Hills Road. In the back of this property is a natural prairie that is like what the first settlers would have encountered upon their arrival to the area. (Courtesy of Brian Landis.)

Gregory Rumelhart purchased 63 acres on the north side of Harlem Road (Section 27), where Rock Cut State Park is today. This is his son Archie L Rumelhart and his wife, Minnie, in September 1885. They were married on June 25, 1885. Archie was born on December 6, 1855, and died on June 2, 1937. His occupation was listed as farmer, like most of the landowners in the Rock Cut area. (Courtesy of Midway Village Museum.)

Clyde Rumelhart, the son of Archie and Minnie Rumelhart, born on April 23, 1886, is shown here in June 1896. Although the Rumelhart family were holders of just over 100 acres of land in Harlem Township (Section 27 and Section 33), Clyde, like many from the area, went to work in industry. (Courtesy of Midway Village Museum.)

The Harlem town hall (the building to the left) was built in 1873 and stood facing Forest Hills Road. At the time, Forest Hills Road in and around Harlem was called Bluff Street. Harlem Road was called Church Street. The Harlem town hall was moved to Midway Village, where it currently resides. It is one of only three public buildings remaining of the original Harlem Village. The building on the right is Harlem Village School after the first addition was put on. (Courtesy of Midway Village Museum.)

The Harlem town hall is seen here around 1950. When the building was moved, the roof was lowered to accommodate transportation. (Courtesy of Midway Village Museum.)

The Sonneson family owned and operated this store and gas station at the corner of Henry and Forest Hills Roads. This was once the site of the Harlem blacksmith shop. The store was built from timber from the blacksmith shop when it was torn down in 1939. This building was a Subway sandwich shop until late 2018. (Courtesy of Don Sonneson.)

This is another view of the original Harlem Store (built in 1871). When this photograph was taken around 1900, it was owned by the Fabrick family, who also owned the grain elevator in Harlem. (Courtesy of Brian Landis.)

Chris' Antiques at 5152 Harlem Road was the last business to occupy the Harlem Store. This building was erected in 1929 and opened in 1930. It replaced the original store that burned in 1928. It was torn down when Woodward Governor purchased the property as part of their development plan. (Courtesy of Brian Landis.)

This is the Hawley Fabrick home one day before it was scheduled to be torn down in 2013. The home was built by Lewis Fabrick in 1860. The Harlem stockyards stood to the right of where the truck is. (Courtesy of Brian Landis.)

David W. and Emma Jane (Conklin) Evans were married on April 27, 1868. David Evans was a sergeant in Company L, 8th Illinois Cavalry. (Courtesy of Midway Village Museum.)

The David W. Evans farm stood at 7515 and 7519 North Second Street on what was once called Beloit Road. There were two homes built on this property. Both still stand where there is currently a used car lot. The Rockford, Beloit, & Janesville interurban railway once ran in front of this property. The line was decommissioned, and the tracks were removed in 1930. This photograph is from around the 1920s. (Courtesy of Midway Village Museum.)

The David W. Evans farm was named River View Farms. It was a 149-acre parcel in the northwest quadrant of Section 31 in Harlem Township spanning both the east and west sides of North Second Street. It was bordered on the west by the Rock River, hence the name. This home at 7515 North Second Street, as well as the home at 7519 North Second Street, now serve as offices for a used car lot. (Courtesy of Midway Village Museum.)

The North Rockford Motel was built in 1945 at 7820 North Second Street across the street on the west side from River View Farms. This was originally the property of the Ferguson family, early settlers in the 1840s. This is now the Village Inn Motel. (Courtesy of Brian Landis.)

Eva Elnora Sheldon Evans feeds chickens on the Evans farm in 1950. She was the mother of Naomi Huffman, a future Harlem High School teacher. (Courtesy of Jeanine Pumilia.)

Henry Andrus (November 4, 1844–February 2, 1935) was born on this farm to Joel Andrus and Sarah "Sally" Atwood. Henry became an Illinois state representative and then a US senator. He was instrumental in getting funding through for Veterans Memorial Hall in Rockford in 1902. This close-up of the Italian-style farmhouse shows how ornate the home was. Anita Sheldon DeWitte is shown in this 1991 photograph. She is the niece of farm owners Carl and Eva Evans. The last owners of this home were the First Rockford Group in the early 2000s. (Courtesy of Janine Pumilia.)

Pictured are George Calvin "Cal" Evans and Eva (Sheldon) Evans. In the back is Shirley Evans, and on the right is Naomi Evans, who married Hal Huffman in 1940 on the former Joel Andrus farm. After raising a family, Naomi began her career as an English teacher in the Harlem School District. (Courtesy of Janine Pumilia.)

Joel Andrus was born in 1817 to Danial and Minerva (Cole) Andrus. He came with his parents to Harlem Township in 1837 and left for two years to work in the Galena lead mines to help pay for this farm on West Lane Road (Route 173). The Andrus home is pictured deserted prior to being knocked down for development. It sat on the north side of West Lane Road about halfway down the hill from where Showplace 14 is today. (Photograph by Brian Landis.)

One of the oldest farms in the area was the Key Farm at 1024 Harlem Road. The Key family purchased this farm from the Atwood family. Patience Atwood once owed this 100-acre farm. She wrote an 11-page diary about her father, Phinehas Atwood, building the original house in the fall of 1845. The home that stands here now was built in 1947. None of the outbuildings seen in this photograph are still standing. (Courtesy of Vintage Aerial.)

The James Taylor farm sat on Forest Hills Road. Today, the new Subway, laundromat, and Fast Mart gas station are located there. This was Leonard Taylor's birthplace, as well as the birthplace of Erma (Hurlbert) Taylor. She was a school teacher at Free Soil Grade School. (Courtesy of Midway Village Museum.)

25

This is the Lawrence McCarty farm in the northeast corner of Section 29. This is now Polaris Estates. Most of the former farm has been developed, but the farmhouse and one outbuilding are still standing. This image was captured in 1973. (Courtesy of Vintage Aerial.)

The Joseph Yates Farm stood on Section 29 of Harlem Township on the west side of Middle Road (Alpine Road). This is the present site of Sunset Memorial Gardens and Funeral Home. Pictured here around 1910 are Harriet Yates (center) and John Yates (right); the person on the left is unidentified. (Courtesy of Brian Landis.)

Herb Johnson established Sunset Memorial Gardens and Funeral Home in 1952 at 8800 North Alpine Road on the former Joseph Yates farm. This postcard view shows the burial gardens when they were new. (Courtesy of Brian Landis.)

The Joseph Yates farmhouse stood at 8800 North Alpine Road until 1990–1991, when it was razed to make room for Sunset Memorial Gardens. Nothing remains now of the Yates farm. (Courtesy of William L. Johnson.)

Frye's Hi-Way Grocery, seen here in 1938, stood on the northwest corner of Harlem Road and North Second Street in the 8000 block. The store was moved one block to Revere Street to make way for new businesses such as Gene Anderson's gulf station and marina. Frye's provided hot and cold lunches for Harlem Consolidated School students. The owners were Theodore Frances Frye and his wife, Alice Olga Frye. (Courtesy of Rose Bennett.)

This is the Salt and Pepper Shaker Cafe at 7930 North Second Street. It was built as a home and then converted into a restaurant. Here, it is being moved to a new location on Superior Avenue, where it will once again be a private home. (Courtesy of Brian Landis.)

This property once belonged to Charles Haskins, an early resident of Harlem Township. Later, it was sold to Fred W. Rogers. Not long after this photograph was taken, it became the new site of Logli Supermarket (now Schnucks Supermarket). When the Logli store opened in 1998, it was the largest grocery store in the state of Illinois. (Courtesy of Kevin Jacobson.)

29

These were the members of the Harlem Village baseball team in the 1890s. From left to right are Ed Peterson, Asa Taylor, Charlie Parker, Paul Conklin, Faye Davis, Jack Bennet, Herb Conklin, Boyd Easton, Clarence Rogers Charles Key, unidentified, and Harrison Conklin. This photograph was taken east of Forest Hills Road on the south side of Harlem Road across from Harlem Village. (Courtesy of Midway Village Museum.)

Members of the Harlem Village baseball team are pictured in front of the Harlem Methodist Church at 2000 Harlem Road. From left to right are (first row) Asa Taylor, Charlie Parker, Bernie Molaine, and Paul Conklin; (second row) Clarence Rogers, unidentified, Lloyd Easton, unidentified, and Boyd Easton. (Courtesy of Midway Village Museum.)

PARAMOUNT ROLLER RINK

NO, SECOND STREET ON ROUTE 51

Invitation to

PRIVATE SKATING PARTY

Sponsored by _____ Fro O a _____

Date _____ Feb 17, 1941 _____

TIME 7:30 – 11   Phone Parkside 445

No skaters admitted without properly endorsed card

(OVER)

The Paramount Roller Rink was also known as the Paramount Ballroom and Paramount Skating Rink. It offered both public and private skating. Located directly across the street from Harlem Consolidated School, the rink was popular among Harlem Township students. Its popularity was area-wide due to weekend matinees and night-time availability. (Courtesy of Brian Landis.)

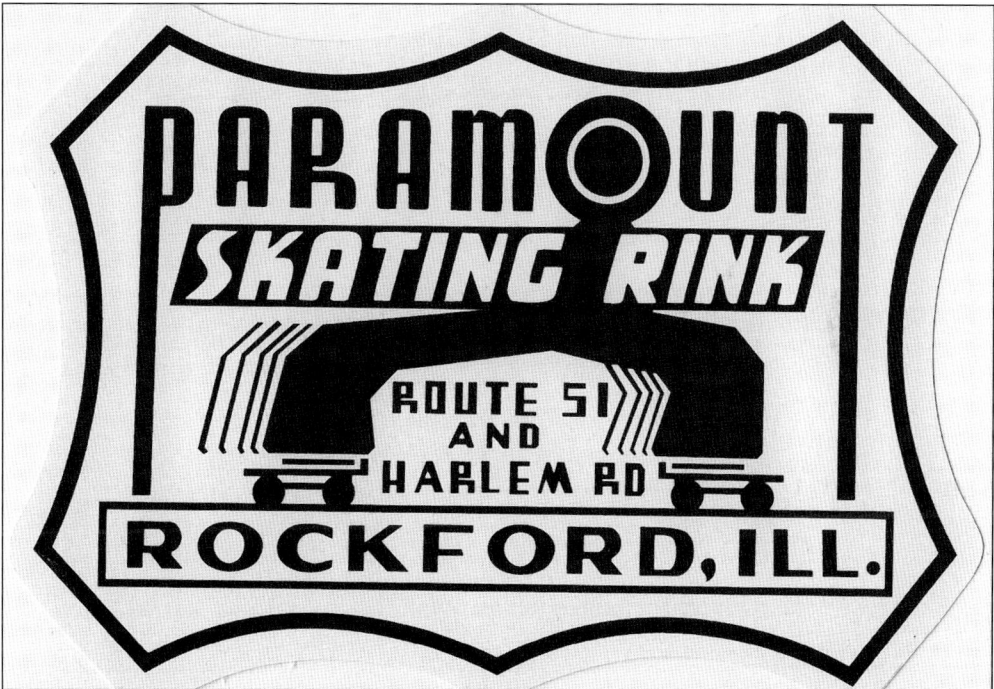

This decal advertises the Paramount Skating Rink at Route 51 and Harlem Road. Because North Park was an unincorporated area, it was often referred to as being in Rockford because of its proximity to the city. This was true of many things in the Harlem Township area, including Rockford Speedway. (Courtesy of Brian Landis.)

ROCKFORD'S FIRST CHAMPIONSHIP

WALKATHON

MARATHON
ENDURANCE CONTEST

PARAMOUNT
BALLROOM

4,000 Comfortable Seats
North Second St. Road — Rockford, Illinois

MASTERS OF CEREMONY

"DUKE" HALL

BILLY LANG   BENNY LEONARD
        MERRITT COOK

BROADCASTING DAILY

WROK   ROCKFORD
           1410 Kilocycles

THREE BROADCASTS -- 11:30 to 11:45 A.M.
5:30 to 5:45 P. M. -- 8:45 to 9:00 P. M.
"DUKE" HALL AT THE MICROPHONE
TUNE IN WHEN YOU CAN'T ATTEND

ADMISSION

MATINEES—15c from 5 A. M. to 5 P, M,
NIGHTS—25c from 5 P.M. to 5 A,M,

The Paramount Ballroom was extremely popular because it broadcast live at least three times a day on WROK and WGN in Chicago. A radio antenna and transmitter were about half a block away on the south side of Harlem Road. On May 20, 1934, Earl Bennet played here live and was broadcast all over Northern Illinois. (Courtesy of Brian Landis.)

This group photograph of walkathon participants was taken on Christmas Day 1933 at the Paramount Ballroom. The ballroom was capable of seating 4,000 people. Beardsley and Piper Division Machine Shop occupied the former Paramount building until it burned down in December 1967. (Courtesy of North Suburban Library.)

The Paramount Ballroom was located in the old Monarch Aircraft Industries building, on the southwest corner of Harlem Road and North Second Street. This is Beverly and Chuck at the Rockford walkathon. (Courtesy of Midway Village Museum.)

On the southeast corner of Harlem Road and North Second Street was the Harlem Safety Park, featuring mock buildings, electric cars, bicycles, and small-scale roads. On the northeast corner was Salamonies Grocery. On the northwest corner was Gene Anderson's gulf station and marina. On the southwest corner, out of view, was Ed Thorne's hardware store and marina. (Courtesy of Vintage Aerial.)

Famous for its Texas burger and Coney dog, this Dog n Suds drive-in restaurant was located at 1421 Harlem Road for over five decades. The gas station east of there was still pumping gas when this photograph was taken in 1973. The building is currently occupied by Molly's Slots. (Courtesy of Vintage Aerial.)

This is Loves Park Auto Parts and Salvage Yard, located at 9902 North Second Street. The Prairie Moon Saloon can be seen at lower right. This aerial photograph was taken in 1973. (Courtesy of Vintage Aerial.)

Two

ARGYLE, ILLINOIS

Pictured here are the Argyle Depot, grain elevator, general store, and the Argyle creamery. The Argyle Depot was served by the CNW Kenosha Division Line. Today, the Bach Timber & Pallet Company is located at the site of the former grain elevator and Argyle Depot. Argyle was founded by the Armour brothers, the Greenlees, and the Reids. (Courtesy of Brian Landis.)

This was the Argyle Post Office in 1915, when C.H. Thornton was the postmaster. (Courtesy of Midway Village Museum.)

This is the original Greenlee farm on the north side of West Lane Road, just east of where Interstate 90 is today. This is a rare photograph of an early settler home. James Greenlee and his wife, Margaret, immigrated to the United States in 1842 from Scotland and settled in Harlem Township on the first homestead. The man and woman shown here are thought to be Peter and Elizabeth Greenlee; Peter was the son of James Greenlee. (Courtesy of Robert Ralston.)

This is a rare winter view of horses and a carriage on the Greenlee farm on the north side of West Lane Road near where I-90 runs today, just east of Rock Cut State Park. The nearest town to get provisions would have been Argyle, about two miles away. (Courtesy of Robert Ralston.)

This creamery in Argyle was organized and licensed in 1884. It was located on the south side of Main Street and manufactured the Sweet Heather brand of butter. In 1917, the home and creamery were sold to Union Dairy of Rockford for $2,000. The creamery was abandoned in 1930 and burned to the ground in the 1970s. (Courtesy of Brian Landis.)

Elizabeth Greenlee of Caledonia married James Greenlee of Harlem on November 21, 1895, in Argyle, Illinois. (Courtesy of Midway Village Museum.)

This is the wedding photograph of Janet "Nettie" Ralston and Robert Greenlee. They were married on February 15, 1894. (Courtesy of Midway Village Museum.)

Laura M. (Greenlee) McDonald was the daughter of James and Elizabeth Greenlee, born on March 27, 1897. She was a teacher in Harlem Township before moving to Los Angeles, California, where she died on February 3, 1954. Sitting in the automobile is her husband, John P. McDonald, also of Harlem Township. He became a salesman in Glendale, California. (Courtesy of Robert Ralston.)

This is the inside of the Billy Bell grocery store in Argyle. (Courtesy of North Suburban Library.)

BILLY BELL
General Merchandise
"Good Goods The Year Round"
Argyle, Illinois

This is the back of the Argyle grocery store in the late 1950s. The store was owned by Harold Jackson, who purchased it from Billy Bell. The automobile is a 1954 Buick convertible. (Courtesy of Don Herdenreich.)

This is the Ralston farm on the north side of Harlem Road close to the curve, where Harlem Road turns into Argyle Road. The farmhouse is gone today, but the outbuildings are still standing. (Courtesy of Robert Ralston.)

One of the Paulsons (probably Warren) cuts grain on an early Farmall tractor with a John Deere umbrella. Farmall tractors debuted in 1924 and lasted until 1973, when International Harvester dropped the name. This photograph is from around the 1940s. (Courtesy of Jennifer Paulson.)

Warren and Wayne Paulson stand in front of the Paulson silo and barn with a huge corn stalk for 4-H. Between 1935 and 1941, the Paulson farm played host to a very popular Saturday-night barn dance. It featured live music and food, and could draw 600 or more people every Saturday night from July to October. The barn seen here was built in the spring of 1935 after a devastating fire leveled the first barn on November 15, 1934. Warren Paulson later turned it into the Paulson Museum. (Courtesy of Jennifer Paulson.)

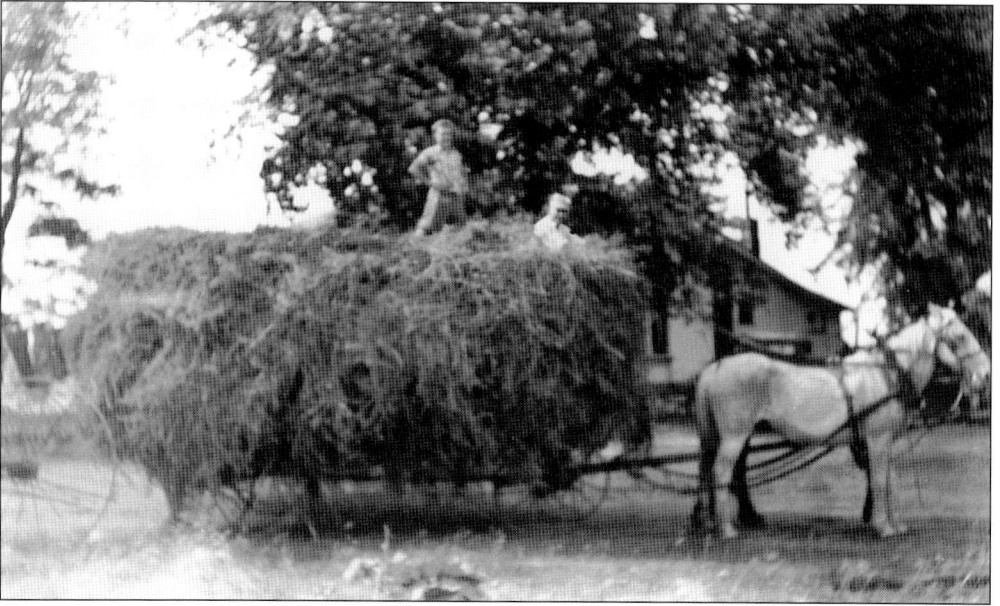

This is Warren and Donald Paulson on the Paulson farm around 1934. Warren was born on the farm on July 14, 1922, and died on November 28, 2012. He was well known in the Harlem Township area. Donald was born in 1921 and died in 1990. Horses were still being used on some farms in the area until after World War II, when farm equipment manufacturers stopped making horse-drawn implements. (Courtesy of Jennifer Paulson.)

The Scottish Cemetery, also known as Argyle Cemetery and Scotch Argyle Cemetery, is half in Winnebago County and half in Boone County. For that reason, the road changes from Picken Road to Cummings Road in front of the cemetery. (Courtesy of Vintage Aerial.)

Three

RAILROADS AND MINING

This view of the CNW Kenosha Division line looks northeast toward Alpine (crossing along the tree line). The house and outbuildings on the left are where Windsor Lake would be after the area was quarried for sand and gravel. This spot is where the KD line first entered Harlem Township from the south. This photograph was taken in 1937, not long after the removal of the KD line. Fences have already been built over the crossing. (Courtesy of Roy Peterson.)

This view of the KD line looks northeast toward the village of Harlem from where it crosses Forest Hills Road. This is approximately where Forest Hill Court is today. At center in the foreground is the J.H. Patterson building. (Courtesy of Roy Peterson.)

This photograph was taken in 1936 of the Harlem Depot and a portion of the Patterson Lumber Company. The CNW Kenosha Division line passes between them. During World War I, the bodies of local servicemen killed in action were left here at the Harlem Depot for families to retrieve. (Courtesy of Brian Landis.)

This photograph of the Harlem Depot and J.H. Patterson Lumber Company was taken in 1937. The sign on the Harlem Depot had already been removed and saved by Ward Fabrick. It is still in existence. Shortly after this, the depot was razed. The last thing to go in this photograph was the J.H. Patterson building, razed in 1942 after 54 years of service. (Courtesy of Brian Landis.)

This was the stockyards at Harlem Village on the property of Ward Fabrick. The small stockyard building on the left was the last to survive, lasting until 2012. The hills in the background are now Forest Ridge Subdivision. (Courtesy of Midway Village Museum.)

This view of the former KD line faces north. The J.H. Patterson building was formerly the Harlem grain elevator, owned and operated by the Fabrick family. To the right across the tracks is where the Harlem Depot stood. When this photograph was taken in July 1937, the depot had been removed two months earlier. Just beyond the stand of trees, the KD line made a sharp turn to the east toward Rock Cut. (Courtesy of Roy Peterson.)

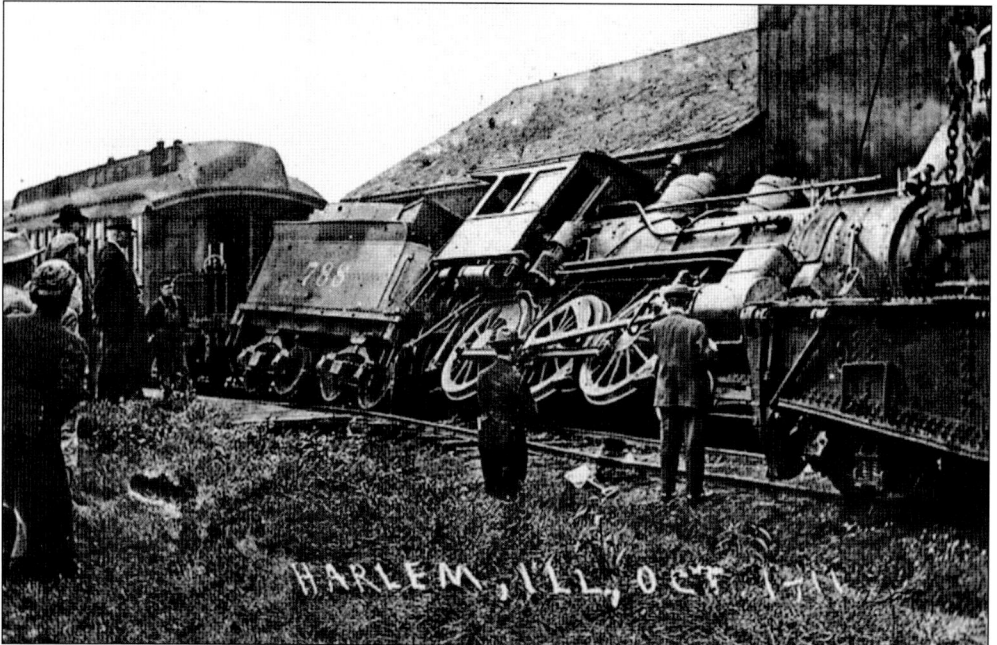

This derailment of a CNW train on the KD Line occurred on October 1, 1911, in Harlem Village. Standing to the left with her back to the camera is Emma Taylor Hurlburt. The number of trains varied on this line, but in 1895, the KD ran 10 trains per day. (Courtesy of Brian Landis.)

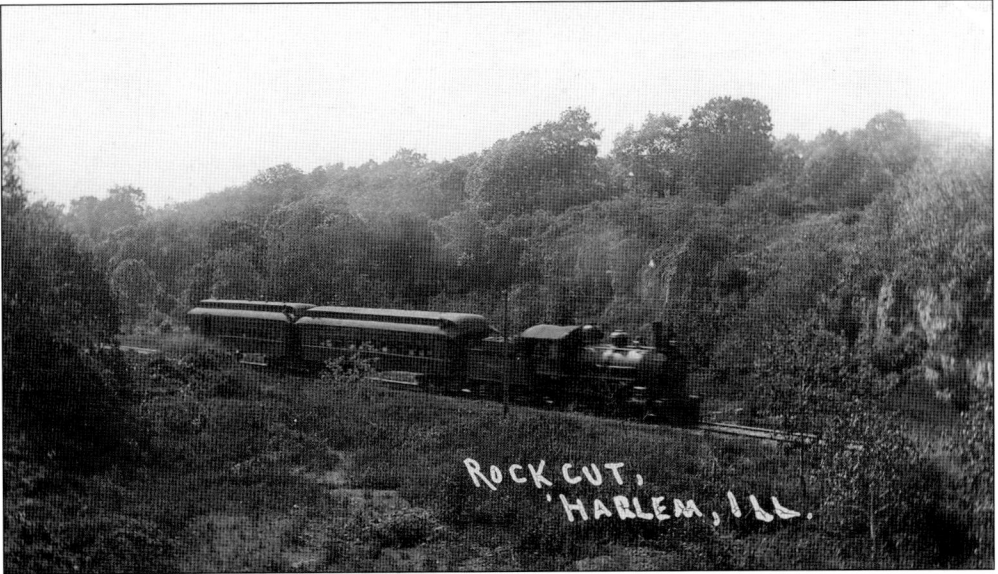

A Rogers 4-6-0 locomotive passes through what is now Rock Cut State Park in 1916. The train is heading toward Argyle with a combine car in the rear. Combine cars were used for both freight, passengers, and sometimes mail. Most of the trains that passed through Harlem Township were not large, even by the standards of the day. (Courtesy of Brian Landis.)

The limestone bluffs on the left are where Rock Cut gets its name. In 1859, the Kenosha & Rockford Railroad (originally the Kenosha, Rockford & Rock Island Railroad) began plans to cut through the limestone in what is now Rock Cut State Park. By 1861, now owned by the Chicago & North Western Railroad, the company had cut through these buffs for the railroad right-of-way. (Courtesy of Roy Peterson.)

Once in Rock Cut, the KD line passed through what is now Pierce Lake. The area shown here is all underwater now except for the mound at right, which sticks out just above the surface of present-day Pierce Lake. (Courtesy of Roy Peterson.)

This KD line bridge crossed Willow Creek where present-day I-90 is. This view looks east toward Argyle. Cows can be seen grazing in this June 11, 1937, photograph. (Courtesy of Roy Peterson.)

Moving east toward Argyle in July 1937, these rails were still in place. The tracks were removed in 1937 from west to east. In the early 1860s, steam engines were relatively small. As engine weight increased, the rails were upgraded. Seen here is the 60-pound lightweight rail that the KD line originally used. This lightweight rail prevented large steam engines of the day from running on the Kenosha Division of the CNW. (Courtesy of Roy Peterson.)

There were still railroad cars on the KD line west of Argyle in 1937. Here, the sign indicated to railroad crews that Argyle was one mile away. (Courtesy of Roy Peterson.)

Passengers await the CNW KD line train at the Argyle Depot prior to passenger service being stopped in 1931. Freight, milk, and other goods continued until May 1937, when the line was decommissioned. (Courtesy of Brian Landis.)

These boxcars are facing west in Argyle in 1937. The sign on the Argyle Depot at center is already gone. The grain elevator burned to the ground in the 1970s. (Courtesy of Roy Peterson.)

These gondola cars, pictured in Argyle, spelled the end for the KD line in Harlem Township as they picked up railroad ties. This view is facing east in 1937. (Courtesy of Roy Peterson.)

Former Soo Line 2-6-0 Mogul No. 104, owned by Harry P. Bourke of Escanaba, Michigan, was the work train that took up the rails and ties of the KD line. The line was taken up from the west at Windsor Road to the east at Argyle. It was then taken up farther east through Caledonia. This was during the spring, summer, and fall of 1937. This photograph was taken in Argyle. (Courtesy of Roy Peterson.)

Harlem Consolidated High School children attending the second annual Play Festival at Harlem Consolidated School are boarding and de-boarding a Rockford, Beloit & Janesville electric railway car at Harlem Road and North Second Street on May 13, 1913. This service ran from 1902 and was stopped by 1930. It was one of the principal reasons that Harlem Road and North Second Street was chosen as the site for the new Harlem Consolidated School in 1910. (Courtesy of Brian Landis.)

In 1919, a Rockford, Beloit & Janesville interurban car hit a lumber truck at North Second Street and Harlem Road in front of Harlem Consolidated School. The motorman on the interurban car was killed. (Courtesy of Brian Landis.)

This is a Rockford & Interurban Railway fare receipt from 1926 or 1927 for a ride from Janesville, Wisconsin, to Beloit, Wisconsin, on September 19. The cost of the ride was 45¢. A ride within the Harlem Consolidated School District was 5¢. (Courtesy of Brian Landis.)

ROCKFORD & INTERURBAN RAILWAY CO.

CASH FARE RECEIPT

This is your receipt for fare paid to the station indicated.

Form C. F. R.	79459	HALF FARE ★ PUNCH HERE

From	To	From	To
★ Rockford ★		★ Powers ★	
★ Snow Crossing ★		★ Town Line ★	
★ Pearl Ave. ★		★ Riverside ★	
★ Harlem Road ★		★ Trolleyside ★	
★ Home Acres ★		★ SouthJanesville ★	
★ Ralston ★		↵ Janesville ★	
★ Crandall ★			
★ Hutchins ★			
★ Camp Almond ★		**Amount of Fare Paid** Punch in two Columns when necessary	
★ Roscoe ★			
★ Moore ★		CENTS	
★ Hononegah ★		5	55	105	1
★ Rockton ★		10	60	110	2
★ Shaw ★		15	65		3
★ N. W. Ave. ★		20	70		4
★ Beloit ↷		25	75		
★ Elmwood ★		30	80		
★ Inman ★		35	85		
★ Yost Park ★		40	90		
		45	95		
		50	100		

Jan.	Feb.	Mar.	1	2	3	4	5	6	7
April	May	June	8	9	10	11	12	13	14
			15	16	17	18	19	20	21
July	Aug.	Sept.	22	23	24	25	26	27	28
Oct.	Nov.	Dec.	29	30	31	**1926**	**1927**		

Harlem Township has had many rock quarries. Limestone was used for building foundations at first, followed by roads. Larson Sand and Gravel was a large operation in Harlem Township. From North Alpine Road to Harlem Road was essentially one big quarry operation. By the early 1970s, most of them had been shut down and filled in. This large crane was used to dig the pits. The text on the back of the crane reads "Osage Coal Company." The firm was based in Osage, Oklahoma. (Courtesy of Edwin Carlson.)

These small steam engines were side tank engines—a steam train with water on board as opposed to an engine and tender. They were used in the Larson Sand and Gravel pits to transport sand and gravel out of quarries. The tracks were movable. The gravel pit shown was north of the Alpine and Maple gravel pit and ran parallel to Alpine Road. The sides of this particular pit were not tapered, but instead stood at a 90-degree angle. (Courtesy of Brian Landis.)

This aerial view facing south in 1960 features many known landmarks. At the bottom (north) is Juniper Lane, which still dead-ends at the gravel pit. The next road to the south of the Larson Sand and Gravel pits is Harlem Road. The Harlem Cemetery and Church can be seen, as can the former Bullet Stop Gun Shop farmhouse. This farmhouse was the Asa Taylor farm, built in 1863. The next streets to the southwest are Alpine Road and Maple Avenue (curving around). The area between Harlem Road and Maple Avenue is where the Harlem Alpine Shopping Center is today. (Courtesy of Brian Landis.)

Driving down Windsor Road used to make some drivers nervous because there was water up to the road on the north and south sides. This view looks west down Windsor Road, which is closed because a portion of it gave way due to flooding. The small building on the left was a security office for Larson Sand and Gravel. Windsor Road was still just a two-lane blacktop when this photograph was taken in May 1972. (Courtesy of Edwin Carlson.)

This expansive aerial view shows Windsor Road running east and west at the south (bottom) of the photograph. Between Clinton Road and the railroad tracks, there was a driving range (lower left). Several of the Larson Sand and Gravel pits can be seen, with more just out of view. The Levie Landers farm can be seen on Maple Avenue, as can both of the Fred Rogers farms; one is just south of where the Harlem Alpine Shopping Center is today (along North Alpine Road), and the other is at the corner of Harlem and Alpine Roads. The go-cart track is at center along Clinton Road. (Courtesy of Edwin Carlson.)

The Larson Sand and Gravel pit at Windsor and Alpine Roads became Windsor Lake in 1952. It was very popular for swimming and fishing. Due to electrocutions from underground wires, the lake was closed to swimming in the early 1970s. It has gradually filled in over the years but still remains viable for fishing. (Courtesy of Edwin Carlson.)

Four

MACHESNEY AIRPORT

Fred Machesney was born on March 17, 1898, in Annawan, Illinois. He was the son of Minnie and Henderson Machesney. He volunteered for military aviation service on October 14, 1918, at the very end of World War I. Like many pilots of the day, Machesney was a barnstormer, often doing stunts. He soon realized that there was money to be made from aviation. He purchased 55 acres in Harlem Township and began his own airport in 1927. (Courtesy of the Kewanee Historic Society.)

PVT. F. E. MACHESNEY
ANNAWAN, ILLINOIS

Born Annawan, Ill., March 17, 1898. Son of Minnie and Henderson Machesney. Wife, Mae. Volunteered Oct. 14, 1918. Aviation. Aeronautical Supply Depot. Garden City, L. I., N. Y.

Civic pride should prompt YOU to visit

MILLER FIELD

North Second Street Road, Opposite Harlem School

TOMORROW

to see the first airplane of ROCKFORD MANUFACTURE

Are YOU aware of the progress of this promising new Rockford Enterprise?

Much as aviation has advanced, almost beyond the f u l l conception of the general public, it will enlighten you to understand and to see what the future progress of this new organization means to Rockford. If you haven't been out this way lately you will be surprised to find what has already been done. Come early. Bring the family. Be prepared to spend a very enjoyable as well as educational afternoon.

Come and "C"

Monarch Aircraft Industries, Inc.
Rockford, Illinois

The first Rockford Airport (also referred to as Miller Field) was located at Harlem Road and North Second Street. It was bounded by North Second Street on the east, the Rock River to the west, Harlem Road to the north, and approximately Wallace Avenue to the south. Miller Field was across the street from Harlem Consolidated School. The Rockford, Beloit & Janeville interurban railway ran north and south on the east side of North Second Street. This photograph is from about 1926–1927. (Courtesy of Tim McGrew.)

Miller Field was the hub of early transportation and manufacturing in Harlem Township. Monarch Aircraft Industries Inc. built airplanes at this new industrial site. The plant was not there long, however. The economic crash of October 1929, followed by the Great Depression, brought a quick end to the manufacturing of aircraft. It is not believed that any Monarch Aircraft exist today. (Courtesy of Brian Landis.)

This Curtis JN-4 is one of two airplanes Fred Machesney purchased in 1926 and 1927, the other being the Waco-9. It is pictured at Miller Field (Rockford Airport) just south of where Superior Avenue is today. The building on the right is Harlem Consolidated High School. The two buildings on the left were homes on Harlem Road. They were there until Harlem Road was widened to four lanes. (Courtesy of Midway Village Museum.)

This photograph of Fred Machesney and a Waco-9 was taken in 1926, at what would have been Miller Field. He did not buy this Waco-9 or the land north of Miller Field until 1927. The Waco-9 featured the Curtiss OX-5 engine and typically produced 150-160 horsepower. (Courtesy of Midway Village Museum.)

In 1927, Fred Machesney purchased land that once belonged to the Lewis A. Fabrick family. This home was at 8600 North Second Street. The Fabrick family once raised 400 sheep on this property. In time, Machesney owned 165 acres from North Second Street on the east to the Rock River on the west. This home was moved to Rosoce, Illinois, on North Second Street when Machesney Mall was built here. (Courtesy of Brian Landis.)

The Fred Machesney home was moved farther north up North Second Street when the Machesney Mall was built in 1978. It currently stands on North Second Street in the Roscoe area. (Photograph by Brian Landis.)

On July 8, 1927, the airport that eventually adopted Fred Machesney's name officially became the Rockford Airport. It remained the official Rockford Airport until the Greater Rockford Airport Authority was created, and the former site of Camp Grant was made into an airport. (Courtesy of Midway Village Museum.)

In 1927, Fred Machesney flew 3,000 passengers in this Waco-9 airplane. Here, it sits on the grass runway, waiting for its next flight. (Courtesy of Midway Village Museum.)

This Travel Air W4000 is shown at Fred Machesney's Rockford Airport with several automobiles of the day. Machesney Airport offered free parking. Where the poles are in the background is North Second Street where the Rockford, Beloit & Janesville interurban railway ran, meaning three modes of transportation are visible here. (Courtesy of Midway Village Museum.)

Fred Machesney was a distributor for Travel Air airplanes. Between 1924 and 1929, Travel Air produced more aircraft than any other American manufacturer. In this photograph, Machesney is standing with Ralph Swaby next to a Travel Air 2000 at Machesney Airport in 1929. (Courtesy of Midway Village Museum.)

From left to right are Fred Machesney, Bert "Fish" Hassell, and Ralph Swaby, Machesney's first pilot, who remained with him for five years before moving to Lawton, Oklahoma. Hassell is most noted for his attempt to navigate the great circle route from Rockford to Sweden in 1928. (Courtesy of Midway Village Museum).

The *Greater Rockford* is seen here at Rockford (Machesney) Airport in 1928. Fish Hassell had the idea in 1926 to fly the great circle route from Rockford to Sweden, with a stop in Sondre Stromfjord airport in Greenland. This airplane was a Stinson Detroiter, sometimes referred to as a Stinson SM-1. The plane was modified by Edie Stinson to hold 700 gallons of fuel and a larger oil reservoir. (Courtesy of Midway Village Museum.)

This is a rear view of the *Greater Rockford* at Rockford (Machesney) Airport in 1928. Fish Hassell and his copilot Parker "Shorty" Cramer flew this modified Stinson Detroiter. The modified plane had a fuel tank in the cabin. (Courtesy of Midway Village Museum.)

There were so many people at Rockford (Machesney) Airport on July 26, 1928, and August 16, 1928, that they were spilling into the roadway of North Second Street. Visible here is a Rockford, Beloit & Janesville interurban crossing sign. The track was on the east side of North Second Street. (Courtesy of Midway Village Museum.)

This is North Second Street facing south. The crowds are flocking to the automobile carrying Fish Hassel and Shorty Cramer. The poles to the left are for the Rockford, Beloit & Janesville interurban on the east side of North Second Street. (Courtesy of Midway Village Museum.)

The attempt to fly from Rockford to Sweden was widely publicized and drew crowds from all over the area. It was thought that this flight would do for Rockford what Charles Lindbergh's recent flight had done for St. Louis, Missouri. Here, a crowd gathers around the *Greater Rockford* on the day of the flight, July 26, 1928. (Courtesy of Midway Village Museum.)

The 700 gallons of fuel onboard the modified Stinson Detroiter proved too much. On July 28, 1928, the *Greater Rockford* lifted off, stalled, and then crashed in a cornfield on the west side of the Rock River. Hassell and Cramer were not injured, but the plane was damaged. After repairs were made, a second attempt was made on August 16. (Courtesy of Midway Village Museum.)

After taking off on August 16, 1928, from Rockford Airport, the *Greater Rockford* was in the air for 24 hours when Bert Hassell had to make an emergency landing on the Greenland ice. The plane remained there until 1969. (Courtesy of Midway Village Museum.)

In June 1969, the *Greater Rockford* was brought back to the United States from Greenland. After a complete restoration from 1978 to 1988, it was put on display at Midway Village and Museum, where it remains today. (Photograph by Brian Landis.)

Fred Machesney purchased this five-passenger Fairchild FC-2 cabin plane in May 1928. It was built in 1927. This began his foray into multi-passenger air service. In 1928, he transported 5,000 passengers around the Rockford area and the Midwest. This photograph was taken in 1930. (Courtesy of Midway Village Museum.)

During World War II, military aircraft were a common sight at Machesney Airport. These planes are lined up in a row with military personnel present. In addition to training aircraft, Machesney Airport was also a stopover for fighter planes during the war. In addition, Machesney also trained WASPs (Women Airforce Service Pilots), who ferried aircraft from manufacturing facilities to forward air bases. The first Rockford-area WASP was Solange D'Hooghe in 1941. (Courtesy of Midway Village Museum.)

This is an Army pursuit aircraft used for training at Machesney Airport during World War II. These aircraft were designed for speed. The Army referred to them as pursuit planes while the Navy called them fighters. In 1947, the pursuit designation was dropped in favor of fighter. Fred Machesney trained 1,139 military pilots from 1939 to 1943 at Machesney Airport. (Courtesy of Midway Village Museum.)

In addition to offering military pilot training, Fred Machesney helped thousands of students obtain their pilots' licenses. This is an advertisement for flight training at Machesney Airport, offering a complete course for only $200. By the 1960s, prices had increased; Machesney Airport was offering flying lessons for $12 per hour, using 1939 Aeronca Champs as trainers. (Courtesy of Midway Village Museum.)

Brothers Jim (left) and Dale Landis are at the site of a small airplane crash at Machesney Airport around the early 1960s. (Courtesy of Barb Speiser.)

On July 14, 1966, a tornado touched down at Machesney Airport. There were five hangars at the airport in that year: four larger ones and one smaller one. All sustained damage to some degree, and three were destroyed. (Courtesy of Linda Sonneson.)

Some planes were broken in two from being thrown through the air by the force of the tornado. (Courtesy of Linda Sonneson.)

An airplane sits on top of a demolished hangar at Machesney Airport on July 14, 1966. This tornado is still one of the most memorable events in Machesney history, forever etched in the minds of those who witnessed the destruction. Just nine months later, on April 21, 1967, a tornado outbreak devastated Belvedere and Oak Lawn, Illinois. (Courtesy of Linda Sonneson.)

This 1973 aerial view of Machesney Airport shows the Fred Machesney home at center. Slightly to the southwest were the airport offices. To the right (south) is the Huskies Drive-In Root Beer Barrel. In 1974, Machesney Airport closed. Not long after, Huskies also closed. Both of these closings marked the end of an era for Harlem Township. (Courtesy of Vintage Aerial.)

Fred Machesney (left) and Nick Rezich stand in front of a 1928 Travel Air WD4000. This would be Machesney's last ride. Although Machesney Airport had been officially closed since 1974, this flight, to commemorate the dedication of Machesney Mall, was the final takeoff and landing there. (Courtesy of Jim Rezich.)

Fred Machesney (left) and Nick P. Rezich hold an OX-5 Banner. OX-5 was the name of a flying club that Machesney sponsored. He and Nick P. Rezich were members. In 1977, Rezich was president of the club. The name is taken from a historic V8 aircraft engine, the first mass-produced aircraft engine in the United States. (Courtesy of Jim Rezich.)

Five

SCHOOLS AND CHURCHES

Andrew J. Lovejoy was born on December 5, 1845, in Section 9 of Harlem Township. At age 21, he left the family farm and went into wholesale sales, engaged in livestock breeding on an international level. He was appointed to numerous public positions, especially those related to county fairs, agriculture, and livestock. He attended schools in Harlem Township and later had a school district (No. 49) and a school named after him. He became supervisor of Harlem Township 1896 and held that position for five years. He died on November 19, 1919. (Courtesy of Harlem Township.)

This is the original Lovejoy Grade School. There would be two more buildings with the Lovejoy name where this school stood. (Courtesy of Harlem School District.)

This is Mrs. Loyd's fourth grade class at Lovejoy Grade School in 1943. Iva Hansen is in the first row, fourth from left. While Lovejoy's attendance was typically smaller than other grade schools in the Harlem District, it played an important role for students who lived on the northern boundary of District No. 122. So much so that a farmhouse was purchased and remodeled into a new school in 1931 to replace the original. Later, another building (the brick building shown here) was added to this site. The two buildings operated until 1960. (Courtesy of Iva [Key] Hansen).

Harlem Consolidated School District was brought about by merging four different districts: Lovejoy (No. 49), Burner (No. 52), Free Soil (No. 56), and Union (No. 61). The Burner School, seen here, was at the southwest corner of Route 173 (West Lane) and Alpine Road. Today, it is the site of Lowes. (Courtesy of Brian Landis.)

This is the original Harlem Village School that was built in 1871. At left, behind the school, is the Harlem town hall. This school would be added to at least twice in its history. Most of these early schools served more than one role. They also served as community centers and sometimes even churches. When built, the front of the school faced Harlem Road. (Courtesy of Midway Village Museum.)

The first addition to Harlem Village School made the school face Forest Hills Road. This addition in 1952–1953 added rooms and changed the character of what was once a typical one-room school. Harlem Village School (District No. 55) was not part of the original consolidation effort in 1910. It was annexed into Harlem District No. 122 by state law in 1953 and reopened in 1954 as Rock Cut School—Harlem District No. 122. (Courtesy of Brian Landis.)

Husband and wife Joseph and Maria Hall are shown at their residence on the south side of Henrey Street in Harlem. This building, constructed in 1852 and later converted to a home, is thought to have been called Sugar Loaf School. It is interesting to note that the village of Harlem was not officially located here in 1852. Schools were often placed at one-mile intervals. Harlem was not relocated here until approximately 1859, when the railroad came through. (Courtesy of Midway Village Museum.)

This is a Harlem Village School class photograph taken in 1896. In the second row on the far left is Clyde Rumelhart. Peering through the glass windows are presumably the teacher and parents of some students. The students in 1896 obtained water from a well a block east of the school. Every day, two students would go down to the well and draw water into a bucket for the others. They all drank from the same ladle. (Courtesy of Midway Village Museum.)

This is the Harlem Elementary and Junior High School fourth-grade class in 1929. When Loves Park Grade School on Grand Avenue in Loves Park was expanded, most of the elementary students were moved there. This left Harlem Consolidated primarily a high school; however, there were parents of students in the northern part of District No. 122 who wanted their children to attend school closer to home. For that reason, there were still a few elementary grades taught here. (Courtesy of Brian Landis.)

B.A. Hoffman replaced Irving Pearson in 1927 as District No. 122's chief administrative officer. In 1969, B.A. Hoffman Middle School was named after him. This illustration of him hung on the wall at Hoffman Middle School for many years. It, like most of the schools in the Harlem District, has undergone many changes. The school will once again be idled in the 2019-2020 school year. (Courtesy of Brian Landis.)

This photograph was taken inside the Harlem Village School at Forest Hills and Harlem Roads in 1939. The teacher is Hazel (Lundgren) Ralston. A Christmas tree adorned with tinsel is on the left, indicating it was probably December. (Courtesy of Hazel Ralston.)

All eight grades are shown in this Harlem Village School photograph from 1935. These students are in front of the new entrance to the school, which now faced Forest Hills Road. The original building faced Harlem Road. (Courtesy of Brian Landis.)

In 1961, voters in Harlem School District approved a $1.8 million bond issue that allowed improvements to Harlem High School on Windsor Road. But this bond issue also supported building a new junior high school along North Second Street just north of Roosevelt Road. It was named Benjamin Franklin Junior High School, known in the area as "Franklin." The school is directly across from where Machesney Airport and Machesney Mall were. (Courtesy of Vintage Aerial.)

Ralston Elementary, at 710 Ralston Road, opened its doors in 1958. The baby boom generation created a need for more schools at an unprecedented rate. (Courtesy of Vintage Aerial.)

North Park Elementary School, at 808 Harlem Road, was erected at the same time as Windsor Elementary School, at 935 Windsor Road, in 1953. Noticeably absent is the Elm Avenue extension that now runs just east of the school. Also to the east is the Key farm. The northeast corner of the Harmony Grange Hall is at lower left. (Courtesy of Vintage Aerial.)

This is an early view of the Harlem Consolidated School. It was built in 1910 for $17,000 and dedicated in 1911. The windows on the bottom were basement classrooms. The windows at the top center were the attic. The school was initially built with four classrooms. One of the key selling points of the new consolidated school was the Rockford, Beloit & Janesville interurban, which ran along North Second Street in front of the school. (Courtesy of Brian Landis.)

Apple trees are being delivered at Harlem Consolidated School in 1915. When the school was finished in 1911, there was a concerted effort to landscape the grounds. The plan was undertaken by Louis Brandt under the direction of J.C. Blair, professor of the horticulture department at the Illinois College of Agriculture. In addition, 100 shrubs and flowers were donated by Buckbee Seed Company of Rockford. (Courtesy of Brian Landis.)

This Harlem agriculture and gardening contest was held in 1912 for the first time and became a tradition. The building behind the students was a small barn built for the students' horses. It was constructed from remnants of Free Soil School, the first school on the southeast corner of Harlem Road and North Second Street. (Courtesy of Midway Village Museum.)

This is 11-year-old Charles McCarthy at a plowing match at Harlem Consolidated School. Agriculture was part of the core curriculum from 1912 until the early 1940s, when Harlem finally dropped it. The encroaching urbanization of the area made agriculture obsolete in the district. This plowing contest was held on the David W. Evans farm adjacent to the school. (Courtesy of North Suburban District Library.)

Agriculture was a big part of Harlem Consolidated's curriculum. Harlem conducted experimental agriculture and did soil testing for local farmers in the high school science laboratories. Starting in 1912, Harlem began a gardening and plowing contest in the field south of the school, where the east side of Superior Avenue is today. These contests were sponsored by Harmony Grange. (Courtesy of Brian Landis.)

This wooden swing adorns the playground in the back (east side) of Harlem Consolidated School. It was built for the younger students by older Harlem students in the mechanical shop classes. This photograph dates to before the second-floor addition was added in 1918. (Courtesy of Brian Landis.)

This is Bessie Wier's primary grade class at Harlem Consolidated School. Wier was a graduate of Central Illinois State Normal School in Normal, Illinois. At that time, there were still teachers in some districts who were teaching with high school diplomas. Wier was making $60 a month when she was hired in 1911. Clifford Burns, a high school teacher and principal of Harlem Consolidated School, made $100 per month. The lighting in this schoolroom was gas. (Courtesy of Brian Landis.)

These students are from the Harlem High School class of 1934. This is a photograph from a yearbook that was put together by the students. There was no money to have professional yearbooks made, and most students could not have afforded them anyway. All things considered, they did a remarkable job. (Courtesy of Brian Landis.)

The second-story addition proved practical, but there was also an architectural enhancement. One of the most prominent features of the remodeling in 1918 was the front facade. The new arched entranceway and tower became iconic features of the school and were featured in many yearbooks. This photograph was taken in 1947 and appeared in the 1948 Harlem *Meteor* yearbook. (Courtesy of Brian Landis.)

This view of Harlem High School in 1934 offers quite a contrast to the original school that was constructed in 1910. In 1918, the 50-ton slate roof was raised, adding a second story with four additional classrooms and additional storage. In 1928, the entire school was gutted and remodeled under B.A. Hoffman. This made the school more efficient and doubled its capacity. (Courtesy of North Suburban District Library.)

Harlem Consolidated School's eighth-grade graduation class of 1920 is seen here. Some of the students shown are Loyal Anderson (first row, third from left), Fred Collins (first row, third from right), and Robert E. Burden (first row, far right). (Courtesy of North Suburban District Library.)

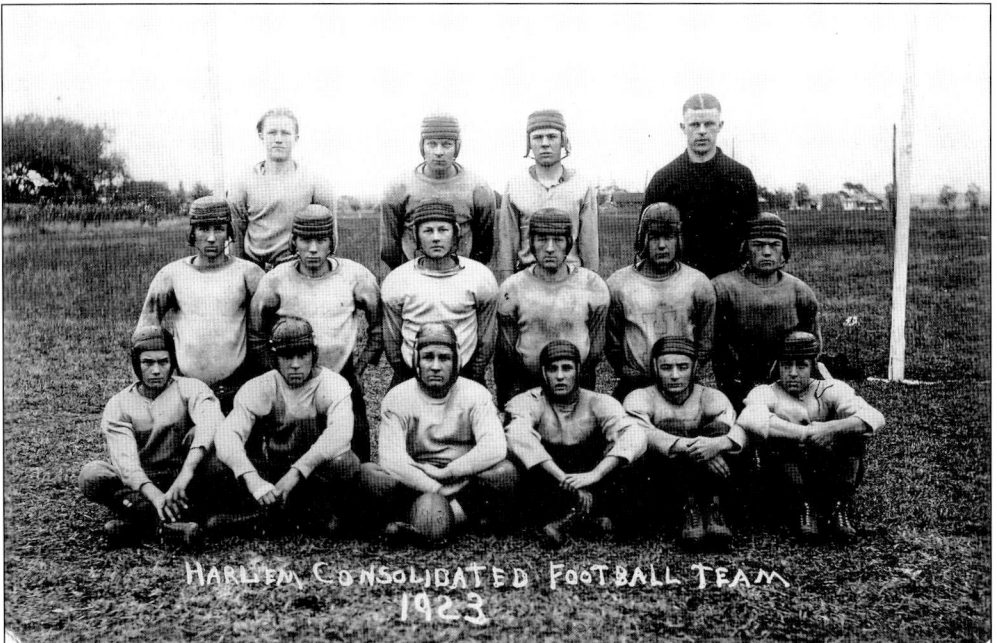

This is the Harlem Consolidated High School football team in 1923. The photograph was taken on the east side of the building in the back of the school. Harlem Road is on the left and was still largely a rural road. This is the Hamilton Shopping Center today. Note the leather helmets of the period. (Courtesy of Brian Landis.)

This photograph of the Harlem Consolidated High School basketball team taken in 1934 has a backstory. There was no money in 1934 for a professional yearbook to be published. This picture was in a yearbook that the students made themselves. It more akin to a scrapbook, but is very well done. (Courtesy of Brian Landis.)

The Harlem High School football team poses on the southwest corner of the school in 1935. In 1928, Harlem joined the Little Five Conference, which was comprised of South Beloit, Honenegah, Pecatonica, and Winnebago schools. There seems to have been an improvement in helmet design in the 12 years since the 1923 photograph. (Courtesy of Brian Landis.)

The 1932-1933 basketball team at Harlem High School is pictured here. Few schools in the Depression era maintained sports programs. The Harlem District, although desperate for finances, chose to keep its programs active. That was remarkable, considering the devastating economic conditions. (Courtesy of Brian Landis.)

Home Coming
Alumni Banquet and Dance
HARLEM GYM
October 5, 1935

6:30 P. M.   Admission 75c

Harlem High School students today host functions for all past Harlem alumni. These are usually informal social gatherings. It was a little different in 1935, when homecoming alumni gathered at the Harlem High School gym. This one was held on October 5, 1935. (Courtesy of Brian Landis.)

88

HARLEM CONSOLIDATED HIGH SCHOOL

Please Do Not Fold
Return Within One Week

LAST NAME: Chamberlain, **FIRST NAME:** Gerald

SCALE OF RANKING
A + Passed with Special Honor 95 to 100
A Passed with Honor 90 to 95
B + Passed with Credit 85 to 90
B Passed 80 to 85
C Near-Failure 75 to 80
D Failure, Lower than 75

School Year 36-37 CLASS IV	Days absent	Times Tardy	English IV	Hist. Amer.	Gen. Science	Shorthand	Typewriting	Civics	Signature of Parent
1.	½	3	C	D	C	C	C	B+	B. Chamberlain
2.		3	A	B−	C	B	C+	A	B. Chamberlain
3.	2		B	C	B	C	B+	A	B. Chamberlain
Class Av.			90	83	86	85	87	93	
EXAMS.			84	87	93	91	92	84	
Final			90	84	87	86	88	93	
1.	½		B	B	C	D	A−		B. Chamberlain
2.	3½	2	B+	C−	B	B	A−		B. Chamberlain
3.	2½	7	A	C−	C	C	A−		
Class Av.			93	83	87	87	93		
EXAMS.			94	88	86	98			
Final			94	84	87	89	93		

This 1936-1937 school year report card belonged to Gerald Chamberlain. It is interesting to note the variety of subjects offered. (Courtesy of Jackie Chamberlain.)

Gerald Chamberlain's high school diploma was quite an accomplishment. About 24,000 schools in the United States closed by 1934 due to the Great Depression. Roosevelt's New Deal, the Works Progress Administration, and the National Youth Administration helped educate over a million people during the Great Depression. Schools in the Harlem District were fortunate—there were no closings. Many students, beginning in the 1920s, were leaving the family farm for factory jobs. It was recognized that getting a high school diploma helped in that endeavor. This diploma was awarded on June 10, 1937. (Courtesy of Jackie Chamberlain.)

Harlem Consolidated High School

This Certifies That

Gerald Chamberlain

having completed the Regular Course of Study as prescribed by the Board of Education, is declared a Graduate of the Harlem Consolidated High School, and is therefore awarded this

Diploma

In Witness Whereof, our signatures are hereunto affixed.

Given at Rockford, Illinois, this 10th day of June 1937.

A. W. Tulisalo, PRESIDENT pro tem
Fuskyberg, SECRETARY
B. A. Hoffman, SUPERINTENDENT

BOARD OF EDUCATION SEAL

Argyle School was built in 1922 as the result of the consolidation of the Brown and Argyle School Districts. This school in the new District No. 127 had 29 students in its first year of operation. This photograph of Argyle Consolidated School was taken in 1930 at the onset of the Great Depression. In 1929, teacher salaries were $124 a month. By 1933, salaries had been lowered to $85 per month. (Courtesy of Robert Ralston.)

This is the 1929-1930 class of Argyle Consolidated School. While the names of the students are not known, their story is. Being the children of mostly rural farmers, they would see first-hand the onset and depths of the Great Depression. In 1933, it took a school board decision to purchase "a good used basketball." Unable to care for the school grounds, the board passed a resolution to pay someone "paupers labor" from the county board of supervisors to clean up the schoolyard and grounds. (Courtesy of Brian Landis.)

These West Lane School children are standing on West Lane Road about where I-90 is today. Maggie Greenlee is the teacher. She was born in 1872 and began her teaching career in Winnebago County and Harlem Township in 1893. As for West Lane School, it was annexed into the Argyle School District No. 127 in 1946. (Courtesy of Robert Ralston.)

These West Lane School children are celebrating their fall harvest by showing off what they grew in 1900. (Courtesy of Robert Ralston.)

The first church attendees in Argyle met in the homes of John Greenlee or Andrew Giffen. A church made of logs was erected in 1842. In December 1844, the Willow Creek Presbyterian Church was officially organized, and the first sacrament of communion was served on January 13, 1845. The church shown in this photograph was originally built as a frame building in 1849 and then bricked in 1858. (Courtesy of Brian Landis.)

This is the Argyle Willow Creek Presbyterian Church dedication in 1877, after the second church was finished. (Courtesy of Brian Landis.)

The Willow Creek Presbyterian Church in Argyle is one of the most recognizable buildings in all of Harlem Township. Its architectural prominence is synonymous with the Scottish community of Argyle. This photograph dates to the 1920s. (Courtesy of JoAnn Reid.)

The members of Willow Creek Presbyterian Church pose for a photograph celebrating 75 years of services. This was a two-day event held on June 22–23, 1920. This building was 43 years old when this photograph was taken. (Courtesy of Brian Landis.)

1845   1920

Seventy-Fifth Anniversary

JUNE 22 and 23, 1920

The Willow Creek Presbyterian Church

REV. EDGAR W. SMITH, *Pastor*

ARGYLE, ILLINOIS

For the 75th anniversary of Willow Creek Presbyterian Church, this booklet was printed. It celebrated the church's history from its establishment in 1845 to 1920. Special services were conducted to celebrate the event. (Courtesy of JoAnn Reid.)

The centennial celebration of Willow Creek Presbyterian Church was held on June 22, 1945. The entire congregation poses in front of the building. (Courtesy of Brian Landis.)

The Harlem Road Methodist Church was built in 1870 and opened in 1871. It is still located at 2000 Harlem Road, just east of the intersection of Harlem and Alpine Roads (Middle Road when this photograph was taken) on two acres donated by Asa Taylor in 1845. The Harlem Cemetery is just to the west of the church. (Courtesy of Terry Johnson.)

The Harlem Methodist Church has undergone several name changes in its almost 150 years. The Harlem United Methodist Church moved in 1964 from 2000 Harlem Road to a new location at 8401 North Alpine Road, where it resides today. The current church in the 2000 Harlem Road location is now New Wine Harvest Church. (Photograph by Brian Landis.)

Construction started on North Park Baptist Church at 718 Harlem Road in April 1956. Seen here is the newly poured foundation. This was next door to the Harmony Grange Hall. During construction, which took four months to complete, services were held at Harlem Junior High School. (Courtesy of First Baptist Church of Machesney Park.)

This 1960 photograph shows the North Park Baptist Church beside the local landmark Harmony Grange Hall. (Courtesy of First Baptist Church of Machesney Park.)

This is the first structure built of the new North Park Baptist Church. It cost $35,000 to build. Over the years, the church would be added to extensively. (Courtesy of First Baptist Church of Machesney Park.)

Harmony Grange No. 957 (right center) was first organized in 1874. The first meetings were held in private homes. Later, meetings were held at the Harlem Consolidated School. In 1945, it was decided that a hall was needed. Harmony Grange Hall No. 957 was eventually built and dedicated on January 23, 1949. The new Grange Hall was a community centerpiece for social events, weddings, 4-H, dances, church groups, and many more occasions. (Courtesy of Vintage Aerial.)

The original North Park Covenant Church was called Harlem Covenant Chapel and sometimes referred to as a "basement chapel." It got its start in 1954, and almost immediately, plans were made to expand the church. In September 1956, ground was broken for the new sanctuary. (Courtesy of North Park Covenant Church.)

This is the Harmony Grange Hall (right) at 720 Harlem Road next to First Baptist Church of Machesney Park. This photograph was taken July 22, 2002, one day before the Grange Hall was scheduled to be torn down. (Photograph by Brian Landis.)

The Harmony Grange Hall interior (with the stage in back) is where countless events were held since 1949. This stage was host to plays, weddings, receptions, and other events. The Harmony Grange first met at Free Soil School when it was organized in 1874. It also met at Harlem Consolidated School. (Photograph by Brian Landis.)

On July 23, 2002, the Harmony Grange Hall was demolished in order to expand the First Baptist Church of Machesney Park. (Photograph by Brian Landis.)

This is a postcard of Open Bible Church at 8202 North Second Street, started in 1954 by Pastor Don Lyons, who was the pastor here for 23 years. At its peak, it had 800 attendees and was home to the weekly 30-minute television broadcast *Quest For Life*. The property was sold when the church was moved to 4721 South Main Street in Rockford. It is now home to the Kelli's Market gas station. (Courtesy of Brian Landis.)

This is the Lovejoy Church on Old Ralston Road in 1960 at the corner of North Second Street. This portion of Ralston Road was renamed Old Ralston Road after Ralston Road was realigned. (Courtesy of North Park University.)

Six

NORTH PARK FIRE DEPARTMENT

This North Park Fire Department equipment includes, from left to right, a 1959 Howe International, 1954 Howe Defender, and 1964 Dodge Power Wagon. (Courtesy of North Park Fire Department.)

North Park fire equipment is shown here on June 3, 1961; from left to right are the chief's car, a 1959 Howe International, 1956 Howe Defender, 1956 Howe International, 1954 Howe Defender, 1953 Howe Defender, 1950 Howe Diamond T, and 1947 International Bean. (Courtesy of North Park Fire Department.)

This is the original North Park Fire Department station at 520 Wood Avenue. The fire department started in July 1946 and began operations in January 1947 when it acquired its first engine, No. 1. The unit on the right is an International, and the unit on the left is a Diamond T. (Courtesy of North Park Fire Department.)

The North Park Fire Department has three fire stations, on Wood Avenue, Alpine Road, and Harlem Road. This is the original Wood Avenue station at 520 Wood Avenue. It was just west of the current station and is no longer standing. (Courtesy of North Park Fire Department.)

Standing in front of Engine No. 4 are, from left to right, Ralph Miley, Moony Aronson, Bill Hansler, Al Levy, Gene Williams, and Earnie Rost. (Courtesy of North Park Fire Department.)

North Park Fire Department members are, from left to right, Marge Ray, Lynn Ray, unidentified, Art Greenlee, Bill Hansler, Ralph Hutson, unidentified, and Elmer Rundquist. (Courtesy of North Park Fire Department.)

These North Park Fire Department members stand by the foundation for the new Wood Avenue station. From left to right are Marvin Nelson, Walt Gibbs, Gene Anderson, Tom Goedert, and Ernie Kleinsmith. This photograph, taken during the winter of 1962–1963, was donated to the North Park Fire Department by Bill Nilson. (Courtesy of North Park Fire Department.)

Lynn Ray was the first North Park Fire Department chief, serving from 1947 until November 30, 1974. He retired on December 1, 1974, after 28 years of service. (Courtesy of North Park Fire Department.)

Charles Dahlberg was North Park fire chief from December 1, 1974, to May 1, 2000. He served the fire department for over 50 years, retiring in 2000. (Courtesy of North Park Fire Department.)

Seen here is the North Park Fire Department Harlem Road station, built in 1954. Additional territory was added to North Park's service area in the early 1950s. (Courtesy of North Park Fire Department.)

Pictured here is the North Park Fire Department Wood Avenue station. The second Wood Avenue station began service in 1964 at 600 Wood Avenue. It replaced the first station, built in 1946. It added extra space, an indoor training area, maintenance facilities, and four bays. (Courtesy of North Park Fire Department.)

Seven

ROCKFORD SPEEDWAY

When Rockford Speedway was built in 1947, it was "out in the country." The speedway had its opening night on May 26, 1948. When this photograph was taken in 1973, Route 173 (West Lane) was still very rural. The gravel pit to the west of the track was no longer being mined for gravel but had not been filled in. East of the track are Rock Cut Stables. (Courtesy of Vintage Aerial.)

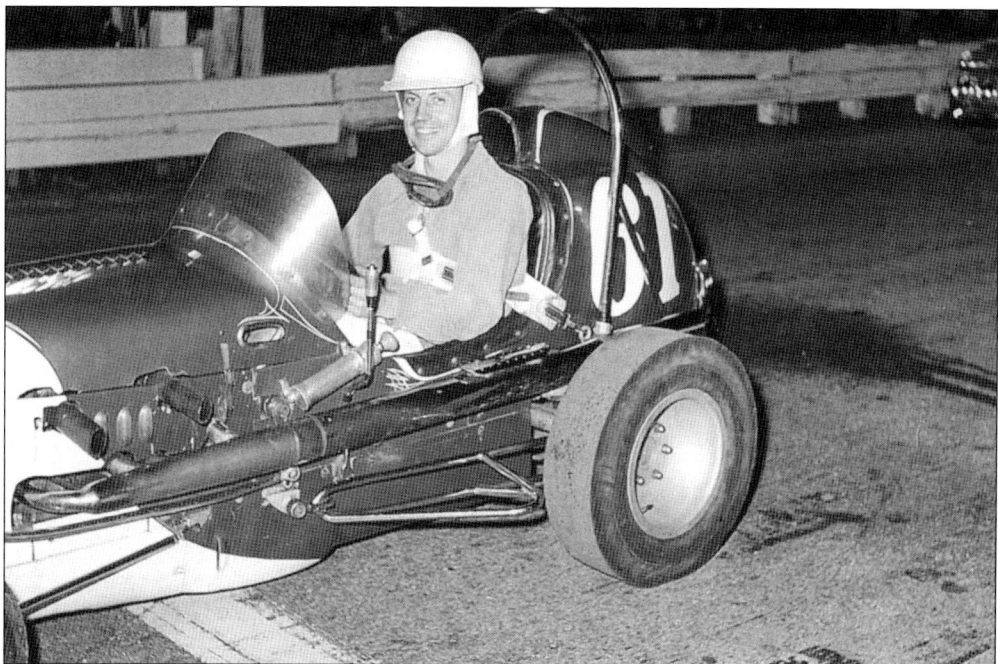

Rockford Speedway originally opened as a midget racing track in 1948. It launched the NASCAR careers of Mark Martin, Dick Trickle, Alan Kulwicki, Ted Musgrave, Rusty Wallace, Rich Bickle, Greg Biffle, Matt Kenseth, Travis Kvapil, Jamie McMurray, Todd Kluever, Erik Darnell, and Scott Wimmer. (Courtesy of Rockford Speedway.)

Kids' night at Rockford Speedway always offered a chance to win something. On this night, the speedway was raffling off a new bicycle. (Courtesy of Rockford Speedway.)

On this day, Rockford newspaper boys were the guests of honor at Rockford Speedway; they are shown here with Hugh Deery. The speedway features special guests or dedicates the night's program to a myriad of groups and causes. (Courtesy of Rockford Speedway.)

Vern Schuh of Loves Park Auto Parts is ready to clean up the next wreck at Rockford Speedway. (Courtesy of Rockford Speedway.)

This is Harlan "Red" Aase, a three-time champion at Rockford Speedway in 1956, 1957, and 1963. Rockford Greenhouses sponsored him in this 1955 Chevrolet. (Courtesy of Rockford Speedway.)

Rockford Speedway has hosted many famous drivers over the years. The champion in 1950, the year this photograph was taken, was Pat Flaherty. He won the 100-lap championship at Soldier Field that year, and went on to race in six Indianapolis 500s. (Courtesy of Rockford Speedway.)

At Rockford Speedway, it is never long until the next crash. Here, track officials are turning a 1940s car right-side-up. (Courtesy of Rockford Speedway.)

There are currently six racing divisions at Rockford Speedway. Some divisions no longer exist or have been renamed along with changes in automobile design. Volkswagens were part of the mini-stock division, which is no longer raced. (Courtesy of Rockford Speedway.)

Joe Shear was an extremely popular driver at Rockford Speedway. He was track champion for six years, from 1967 to 1972. (Courtesy of Rockford Speedway.)

This is Stan Burdick, who, in his 68-year tenure, served as a race official and infield marshal for Rockford Speedway. One of the most recognizable sounds on race night is the sound of an aerial bomb that starts every race program. Stan Burdick lit that bomb for years. His 1955 blue and white Chevy pickup truck was as much of a legend as he was. Burdick died on December 20, 2016, at the age of 90. (Courtesy of Rockford Speedway.)

Eight

ROCK CUT STATE PARK

This rock is arguably the most recognizable feature of Rock Cut State Park. There are a lot of legends about Lone Rock, the name given to this standalone outcrop. Some of the legends date to the Native Americans who once inhabited the area. The last Indian tribe to call this site home were the Winnebagos—latecomers to the region. Early settlers were told that this rock was a ceremonial site, and that there may also have been burial grounds nearby. If the burial grounds exist, they have not been found to date. (Photograph by Brian Landis.)

These students from Harlem Village School are having a picnic in front of Lone Rock in 1909. Dora Hall is the teacher and appears to be accompanied by some of the students' parents. Some of the boys are wearing "Harlem" baseball uniforms. Harlem Consolidated School was still two years away, so these boys were older attendees and baseball players of Harlem Village School. This photograph was taken before Rock Cut was a forest preserve or state park. (Courtesy of Midway Village Museum.)

Pictured is the old Charles Parker home. The property that the Parker farm stood on has tremendous historical value. This was the property that the Buckhorn Tavern once stood on. The Buckhorn Tavern, according to a 1914 newspaper article, was said to be the oldest building in Winnebago County. According to Anna Parker, Indian trails were still present leading off into Rock Cut. The stagecoach made a special trip to the tavern every day due to its popularity. Sylvanus Wade purchased this property from a Mr. Sammons, the grandfather of Anna (Hurlbert) Parker. (Courtesy of Terry Johnson.)

Gertrude (Rogers) Johnson stands in front of the warming station (formerly the Charles Parker home) in Rock Cut State Park. The old home was fitted with new windows, but one year later, it was torn down. It stood in Section 27 of Harlem Township. (Courtesy of Terry Johnson.)

About 200 yards east of the Charles Parker home and this barn is where the Buckhorn Tavern once stood. This barn would have been used to put horses up for the night. The Buckhorn was entered from the south off of Harlem Road. The road went through the Willow Creek area of Rock Cut and then crossed Willow Creek. Almost 180 years later, portions of the original bridge and stagecoach road that crossed the creek can still be seen. (Courtesy of Terry Johnson.)

On the Charles Parker property, there was a large oak tree that showed signs of being augured. The tree stood next to the old Buckhorn Tavern. The holes in this tree were bored by French traders long before settlement in Winnebago County. Clyde and Marge Anderson owned this property when this photograph was taken. They were the last private owners of this property. The barn in this photograph was a hog barn. (Courtesy of Terry Johnson.)

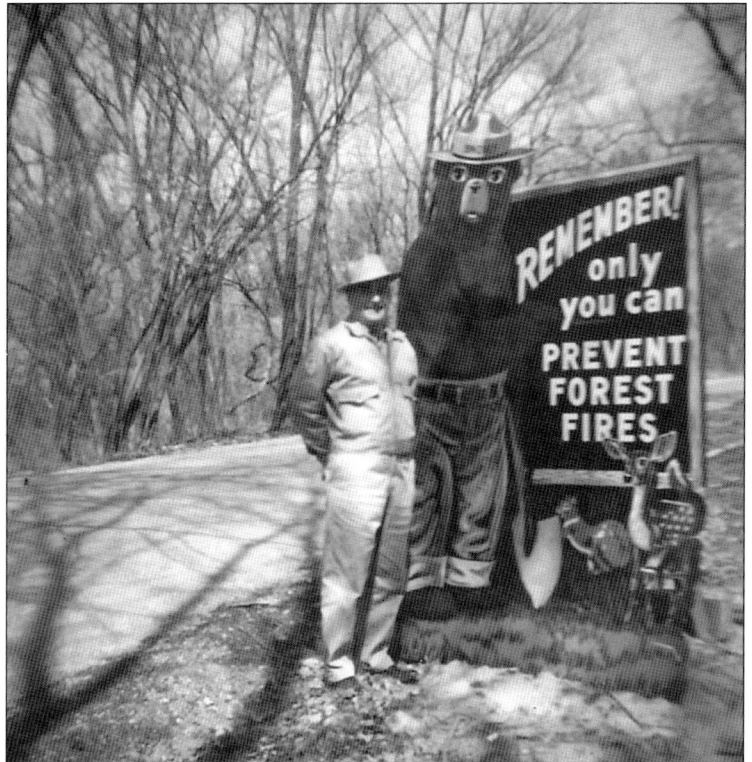

Park ranger Harry Johnson stands at the Harlem Road entrance of Rock Cut State Park. Later on, the Harlem Road entrance was closed, along with the Willow Creek section of the park. The closure forced people to drive around to the new Route 173 entrance. Neither of these changes were popular with locals, but in time, they became the norm. (Courtesy of Terry Johnson.)

The farm of Mathias Ward, often referred to by locals as "Hap" or "Happy" Ward, was one of the last private residences left standing in what would become Rock Cut State Park in the late 1950s. When his property was annexed by the state in 1968, he and his wife lived in a small house on Harlem Road. (Courtesy of Terry Johnson.)

Just months after this March 1962 photograph was taken, water began filling in this region of Rock Cut State Park. This area was formerly pasture for grazing cattle. The fences to keep the cattle in their pasture can be seen at center. (Courtesy of Terry Johnson.)

Another well-known feature of Rock Cut State Park is the spillway. In this July 1962 view, there is one thing noticeably absent: the automobile bridge, which had yet to be constructed. To the left of the spillway were the old Rock Cut campgrounds. These were moved to a different location in the park. The KD line once ran just to the right of where the spillway was built. (Courtesy of Terry Johnson.)

The earthen dam at Rock Cut State Park sprung a leak and had to be repaired. In order to do this, the lake had to be drained. This photograph was taken in September 1970. The large mound at center with people standing on it was to the right of where the CNW Kenosha Division line ran. Portions of the right-of-way were visible when Pierce Lake was drained. (Courtesy of Terry Johnson.)

In September 1970, Pierce Lake was drained; here, one can see the lack of water over the spillway and under the bridge. The lake remained drained until early 1971. Terry Johnson recounts picking up hundreds of fishing lures at this spot while the water was drained. (Courtesy of Terry Johnson.)

These ice sculptures in front of the concession stand at Rock Cut State Park were the result of an ice sculpting contest. This photograph was taken during one of the winter carnivals in the early 1970s. (Courtesy of Terry Johnson.)

These turn-of-the-20th-century campers are having a picnic on the Rumelhart property, once a camping ground of the Winnebago Indians. It was in Section 28 of Harlem Township and is now Rock Cut State Park. (Courtesy of Midway Village Museum.)

When these campgrounds opened, they became an instant success with locals and others from around the region. The campgrounds have been moved from when this photograph was taken in September 1965. People still come from all over the region (including Chicago) to camp here. There are currently 270 spaces for camping at Rock Cut State Park. (Courtesy of Terry Johnson.)

Park visitors are taking a horse-drawn sleigh ride in February 1973. Rock Cut State Park features equestrian trails. (Courtesy of Terry Johnson.)

People here are ice skating on frozen Pierce Lake in January 1973. The Rock River was a popular place for ice skating at the turn of the 20th century. Over time, this ceased. This was an opportunity for another generation to experience the joys of outdoor skating. (Courtesy of Terry Johnson.)

Every sort of sledding has been seen at Rock Cut State Park, including dog sled races. This photograph was taken in the winter of 1973. (Courtesy of Terry Johnson.)

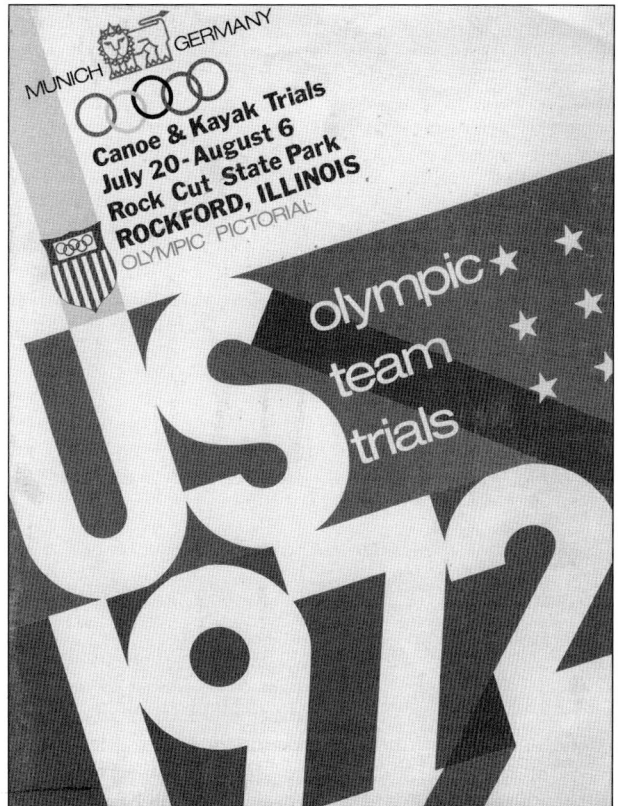

MUNICH GERMANY
Canoe & Kayak Trials
July 20-August 6
Rock Cut State Park
ROCKFORD, ILLINOIS
OLYMPIC PICTORIAL
US
olympic
team
trials
1972

The US Olympic canoe and kayak trials were held from July 20 to August 6, 1971, at Rock Cut State Park for the 1972 summer Olympics. This was a big event for Illinois, Rock Cut State Park, and Harlem Township. The games were watched intently by people in Harlem Township and the surrounding area due to the Rock Cut connection. The Olympics that year were marred by tragedy, though, as 11 Israeli team members were taken hostage and killed by terrorists. (Courtesy of Terry Johnson.)

This is a postcard view of Pierce Lake as seen from the air in 1973. The lake was named after William Pierce. At the top of this view (east) is I-90, and at the bottom (west) is the spillway. The Kenosha & Rockford Railroad bed is submerged. (Courtesy of Brian Landis.)

Pierce Lake is seen here from the shoreline in Rock Cut State Park in an early 1970s postcard. (Courtesy of Brian Landis.)

Harry and Gertrude Johnson pose in front of a tree in April 1938, when Rock Cut was a Winnebago County forest preserve. The valley behind them is now Pierce Lake. They are standing just east of Lone Rock. Today, this area is called Bay View. At the time of this writing in 2019, Gertrude is still alive and 105 years of age. (Courtesy of Terry Johnson.)

Trenedy Johnson, the great-granddaughter of Harry and Gertrude Johnson, stands in front of the same tree in 2013 that Harry and Gertrude stood in front of 75 years earlier. Not visible because of the tree line are some of the same fence posts that are in the 1938 photograph. Behind Trenedy is Pierce Lake. (Courtesy of Terry Johnson.)

Rockford Wing Field and Stream was a conservation club located in Harlem Township on the east side of McFarland Road between Harlem and Nymtz Roads. Harry Johnson, the father of Terry Johnson, was a member. (Courtesy of Terry Johnson.)

From left to right, Terry Johnson, Bruce Sonneson, and Denny Johnson stand on the pier at the Rockford Wing Field and Stream conservation club in the 1950s. (Courtesy of Terry Johnson.)

This was the Lyman Taylor Farm at 2100 Harlem Road, now the oldest surviving home in what was originally part of Harlem Village (when it was moved in 1859.) It dates to 1863. (Photograph by Brian Landis.)

Machesney Park Mall, seen from the air in the early 2000s, opened in 1978 on the site of the former Machesney Airport. It no longer exists as an indoor shopping mall. This is another example of how the center of a community can be dynamic. The center of shopping in Harlem Township is now on Route 173 (West Lane). (Courtesy of Kevin Jacobson.)

The Harlem historical marker was provided by Woodward Govenor and was the work of Muraski Monument of Rockford. It is on the northeast corner of Harlem and Forest Hill Roads and is seen here in November 2016. (Photograph by Brian Landis.)

The Harlem historical marker was a collaboration of several citizens and public officials in Harlem Township and Loves Park, Illinois. Brian Landis (left) stands next to the marker on November 3, 2016. He served as a member of the Harlem Historical Committee and as a historical consultant. (Courtesy of the *Post Journal*.)

DISCOVER THOUSANDS OF LOCAL HISTORY BOOKS
FEATURING MILLIONS OF VINTAGE IMAGES

Arcadia Publishing, the leading local history publisher in the United States, is committed to making history accessible and meaningful through publishing books that celebrate and preserve the heritage of America's people and places.

Find more books like this at
www.arcadiapublishing.com

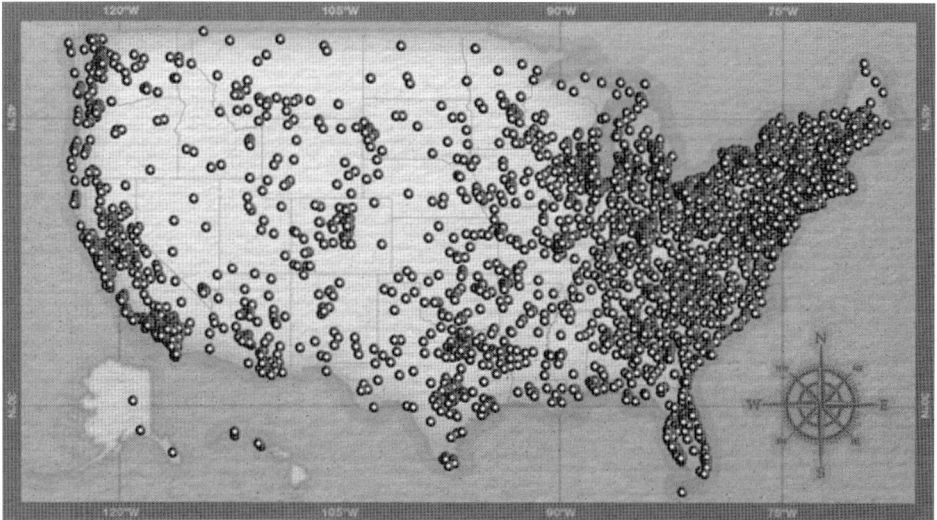

Search for your hometown history, your old stomping grounds, and even your favorite sports team.

Consistent with our mission to preserve history on a local level, this book was printed in South Carolina on American-made paper and manufactured entirely in the United States. Products carrying the accredited Forest Stewardship Council (FSC) label are printed on 100 percent FSC-certified paper.

MADE IN THE USA